The Plays of
Mahasweta Devi

The Plays of Mahasweta Devi

A Critical Study

E. Satyanarayana

Prestige

Published by

Prestige Books

New Delhi 110 058

Ph. 011-25507139

email: prestigebooks@gmail.com

website: asiabookclub.com

Associate Office

60/29-45 Parramatta Road,

Concord, NSW 2137

Australia

ISBN: 81-7551-081-1

Rs. 500

Printed at Chaman Offset Press, New Delhi 110 002

Contents

Introduction
7

***Mother of 1084*:**
Mothers and Rebels
30

***Aajir*:**
Dialectics of Human Bondage
46

***Urvashi O Johnny*:**
The Rebel as Artist
64

***Bayen*:**
A Portrait of the Rebel as Mother
82

***Water*:**
Bhagirath Wins the Battle
104

Conclusion
126

Bibliography
134

Index
141

Acknowledgements

I express my deep sense of gratitude to: Professor A. Jaganmohana Chari, Dean, Faculty of Arts, for his able guidance in the preparation of the present project; Dr. C. Varadachary, Head, Department of English, for his encouragement and advice; Professor S. Laxmana Murthy, Chairman, Board of Studies, for his kind disposition towards me; J. Yellaian, Reader in English, for his constant encouragement; K. Damodar Rao, Lecturer in English, and K. Venkateshwarlu, Asstt. Librarian for providing me with the source materials I was in need of; the staff and the Librarians of Central Institute of English and Foreign Languages and Anveshi Research Centre for Women, Hyderabad, for giving me an access to the source materials in their respective libraries; to Prestige Books for bringing out the book so meticulously and elegantly; and, finally, to my wife E. Sujatha Narayana for her loving support during my twenty-month strenuous research work.

E. SATYANARAYANA

Introduction

Drama, unlike 'novel,' is not new to Indian genius, though it appears to be less popular. India with a variety of cultures, languages and literatures, has a long and glorious dramatic tradition of her own. Drama has been considered 'Fifth Veda' and grouped under the category of the 'Drishya Kavya.'

Indian drama in English is an important branch of Indian English literature though, as K.R. Srinivasa Iyengar points out, "it is neither rich in quantity nor, on the whole, of high quality."[1] The paucity of the good actable plays in English can be attributed to many factors. M.K. Naik observes: "At the outset, there is the fundamental problem of the relationship which constitutes at once a signal advantage and a limitation for drama vis-a-vis other literary forms. Drama is a composite art in which the written word of the playwright attains complete artistic realization only when it becomes the spoken word of the actor on the stage and through that medium reacts on the mind of the audience."[2] Therefore, a living theatre and a live audience are important factors to transform a dramatic work into "a living . . . experience" and it is the lack of these essentials that has hamstrung Indian drama in English all along.[3]

It took a century and a quarter for Indian drama in English to reach a respectable stage and it now challenges comparison with the other forms of literature—poetry and fiction—in terms of quality, if not quantity. The first play in English entitled *Is This Called Civilization*? was written in 1871 by Michael Madhusudan Dutt. Since then, many plays have been originally written in English by "enterprising" Indian writers and many others have been translated into English, in spite of the fact that drama in English fascinated only "the super-sophisticated who live in the cities and the larger towns, in the Universities or in certain Government offices or business houses."[4]

Most of the Indian English dramatists of the pre-Independence period followed the tradition of Elizabethan drama in general and of Shakespeare in particular. As regards the impact of the classical and the Western tradition, M.N. Sundararaman justly states: "Indeed most of the dramatists of the pre-Independence period have been deeply influenced by the classical traditions as also by the characteristics of the popular stage of the folk art. . . . In recent times the influence of American dramatists also has become quite evident. Thus the present day Indian English drama has signs of the influence of two great dramatic traditions—the classical and the Western . . . and among the most recent Indian English playwrights the classical influence is not much in evidence."[5] As such, the major playwrights like Aurobindo, were content to mould their works in the tradition of the West. An urge for freedom of soul and a romantic impulse was also evident in much of their writings with a possible exception of Harindranth Chattopadhyaya who attempted social plays. His *Five Plays* (1937), a collection of social playlets, has been hailed as the "manifestoes of the new realism."[6]

T.P. Kailasam is another dramatist whose plays have been based on the events in the most revered Indian epics, the *Mahabharata* and the *Ramayana*. It appears that unlike Sri Aurobindo and Karnad, "he makes no attempt to interpret old myths to present contemporary problems."[7]

The rich fund of creative power of the playwrights in this period was thus used either to ape the West or to highlight the greatness of the epic characters. M.K. Naik points out that the playwright in English has mostly written "as if he belonged to a race which has never had any dramatic traditions worth the name" (157) and must therefore solely imitate the West.

Interestingly, the element of contemporaneity in drama is evident particularly in the last few decades. In fact, the writer in modern India is disillusioned. He has lost all hopes of seeing the humanity free of all constraints of the modern world. Therefore, he bids good-bye to the worn-out themes so far he has revelled in and now he tries to depict the predicament of modern man with a touch of realism. Indranath Choudhury rightly comments: "After Independence the poet felt a strong sense of frustration because of the presence of disintegration in society and broken relationship with our past heritage. And yet he had coiled beam of hope of a nation and society affluent and flourishing. . . . But with the passing of the time the dream became a hopeless dream and when no fulfilment came till sixties the whole attitude to life took a turn. In the place of frustration, resentment took over. Dreams and values were turned down as romantic sentimentality."[8] What he says here about the concern of the poet is also true of the contemporary dramatist.

However, a concern for the exploited has been found in the Bengali drama. Bengal—"the fountain-head of most forms of Indian English literature"[9]—has paved the way for realistic drama which is committed to the causes—political and social. Earlier, the drama served as an instrument for bringing about awareness among the masses for a change. Playwrights of note have written moving plays depicting the cruelties of the colonial rule and age-old constraints that plagued Hindu society for centuries. It instilled in the reader a sense of urgency and hope—a hope for a bright future for the country. And when drama drifted into the hands of opportunist political parties, it was used as a vehicle of propaganda.

Consequent on the Second World War, there had been innumerable catastrophes that proved to be so turbulent to many a writer who tends "to veer between his sense of belonging to a world community, a common humanity whose spokesman he is and a more specific awareness of his own rootedness among the people he knows best and of whom he writes."[10] The Great Famine of Bengal, which caused the death of millions of helpless rural people, is one of such calamities. Talking about how social realism gained initial momentum in the thirties and how it reacted with particular moral vigour and indignation during this period, K.A. Abbas comments: "It was this large-scale tragedy, which was the crowning crime of British imperialism in India, involving millions of helpless people, that had the profoundest influence on the creative sensibilities of the writers, not only of Bengal, but all over India."[11] As the "true literature stems from a concern with reality as it exists" and a writer must be accountable for his people and times,[12] the writers, inspired by the effects of Bengal Famine, have depicted in their writings the harrowing breaking-down of the humanistic traditions. According to Sarit Kumar Bandyopadhyay, the writers of Bengal, conscious of the socio-economic malaise during this period, "felt a terribly shocking emotional experience which sought to get an outlet in their respective genres."[13]

Around this time, Indian People's Theatre Association (IPTA) was formed by a group of enthusiastic artists of Bengal. This gave a new impetus to the realistic drama. "It took up issues of social abuse, religious bigotry, oppression and economic exploitation."[14] Besides, the movement had revolutionized the whole range of thematic concerns of the playwrights. As Prabhakar Machwe justly points out: "From 1942 to 1945 were the heydays of this movement of exploiting the folk-drama forms and infusing new spirit in these old bottles . . . this movement no doubt helped in bringing about a renaissance in Indian drama. In its content, the drama became more realistic, and the old supernatural, semi-mythical elements were replaced by near-history and economic doctrinaire inevitability, instead of the Fates Historical Necessity stalked the stage blindfolded. In its form the drama is a mirror of the society."[15]

As such, *Nabanna*, a play by Bijan Bhattacharya, presented by IPTA broke new ground both in respect of dramatic content and theatrical form. It describes the miserable plight of the farmers who were forced to migrate, on account of famine, to the metropolis only to be fooled and beggared.

Though the effect of this new dramatic movement was far-reaching and helped in the establishment of the people's theatre, the plays with a genuine ring of social concern and reverberations of realistic themes have rarely been attempted. However, a new dimension is added to the drama, when Mahasweta Devi transforms her stirring stories dealing with the life of the downtrodden into plays. Although she seems to have imbibed the spirit of the new drama movement, her dramatic creation is a class by itself. Her plays, observes Samik Bandyopadhyaya, "in the early seventies confronted Indian mainstream theatre with a challenge—the challenge of an experience revealed—that the theatre failed to take up."[16]

In fact, a brief study of concerns of the contemporary playwrights like Asif Currimbhoy, Girish Karnad, Vijay Tendulkar and Badal Sircar is imperative to show Mahasweta Devi's distinctiveness as a dramatist in the history of Indian drama in English.

The aim of the earlier playwright, as already mentioned, was to write plays to cater to the needs of what could be called "escapist theatre." But the contemporary playwright makes it realistic by portraying the despair arising out of the immediate life around, the complex and intense social order and "a result of this realization was the transformation from romanticism to realism."[17] And the range of the subject matter of the playwright is quite amazing. He draws on history, ancient epics, psychological conflicts, religion and philosophy and contemporary problems.

The field of contemporary Indian drama boasts only of a few writers with a keen eye for the dramatic. Of these, Asif Currimbhoy is one who has to his credit no less than thirty plays which demonstrate his varied interests in the choice of themes. Among the plays with historical and political themes, *Goa* is a two-act play where Currimbhoy deals with a story of passion and violence of the period of the Indian take-over of Goa. The plot is woven around Krishna and Rose, the daughter of Portuguese widow Senhora Miranda. A love affair develops between Krishna and Rose. But Miranda creates a tension in their affair which results in the death of Krishna. However, on the political plane, the scenes in the patio reflect the corrupt atmosphere of Portuguese rule in India and Alphonso's death at the hands of Krishna symbolizes the ultimate collapse of Portuguese rule in India.

The Naxalite Movement, the influx problem of Bangladesh refugees and the travails preceding the emergence of Independent Bangladesh, are themes dealt with in the plays—*Inquilab, The Refugee* and *Sonar Bangla*—which have been fondly hailed as 'The Bengal trilogy.' *Inquilab*, a three act play, throws light upon the origin and development of the revolutionary activities in West Bengal where some agrarian communists opted for violence. In the play, as S.K. Bhatta observes, "Currimbhoy portrays the conflict between the existing order and the new order anticipated between conservatism and the forces of revolution." (99)

While the play, *Refugee* (1971), is concerned with the burning problem of the refugees of Bangladesh who poured into India during the 1971 war, *Sonar Bangla* (1972) deals with another conflict between the people of East Bengal and the Pakistani forces.

Currimbhoy's *Doldrummers* (1960), which was banned for its obscenity, deals with the peculiar life of the lower stratum of urban society. And his *The Dumb Dancer* (1961), a psychological play, tells of a Kathakali dancer who identifies himself with the role of Bhima out and out, and becomes mad. Ironically, the doctor who treats him gets emotionally involved with his problem. In the end, instead of curing him, she herself becomes insane.

Thus, Currimbhoy seems to have evinced much interest in the thrilling and exciting themes. As a result, his plays dealing with political events "have a strong 'documentary' element about them and there is no attempt to understand and project in dramatic terms the ideological implications of the conflicts dealt with."[18]

Unlike Asif Currimbhoy, Girish Karnad, who is one of the leading figures of modern Indian theatre, appears to be taking pleasure in retelling the Indian myth and history. Interestingly, he makes use of the popular folk forms in his dramatic output to tap their springs of vitality with splendid results. His protagonists strive hard to find fulfilment in an imperfect world. As Rajinder Paul says: "In the public or private domain, his characters want to prolong the reign of youth and beauty and defy the conventional bonds of morality and loyalty."[19]

Karnad's *Tughlaq*, the production of which brought him accolades, is a historical play, based on the life of Sultan Mohammed Bin Tughlaq, who was at once a dreamer and a man of action. In the play, Karnad describes the trials that the ambitious king faces in translating his dreams to action.

While his *Yayati* retells the popular Indian theme of responsibility and self-denial, in *Hayavadana,* Karnad deals with the problem of identity by weaving into the play the myth of half-horse and half-man, that hovers between man and god in search of fulfilment. At one level, it is a story of Padmini's love for her two suitors, Devadatta and Kapila, representing mental and physical perfection respectively. But Karnad, by transforming Hayavadana into a complete horse, seems to suggest that "unlike most creatures who adapt themselves to inclement weather or hostile winds, homo sapiens are doomed by their desires to remain unfulfilled."[20]

Vijay Tendulkar's dramatic writings have an element of sex and violence about them. As Veena Noble Dass points out, "he does not consider the occurrence of human violence as something loathsome or ugly as it is innate in human nature."[21] His unconventional probings into the complexities of human existence earned him the fame of being a controversial playwright. However, Tendulkar has dealt sympathetically with women and their problems in most of his plays.

Silence, the Court is in Session, considered to be Tendulkar's best play, exposes the cruelty of modern society in which women are maltreated. Tendulkar has cleverly used the technique of 'play within the play' to bring out the inner agonies of Miss Benare, a character, who is closed in by goblin-like men intent upon tearing her apart in a male-dominated world.

In *Sakharam Binder*, Tendulkar concerns himself with the economic and sexual aggression inherent in our inequitable and repressive society. Sakharam, the Binder, a character, indulges himself in many fornications as to satisfy his quenchless lust. In the end, he is paid back in his own coin when Champa, Sakharam's last match, makes him realize that she wants as much out of life as he does. In fact, here an attempt is made, perhaps for the first time, to bring neglected areas of our common life nearer the theatre.

Unlike the great dramatists mentioned above, Badal Sircar the "dramatist of real promise in the post-sixties literary scene of Bengal," seems to be nearer Mahasweta Devi in his depiction of the sufferings of the oppressed people living in the urban and the rural areas of West Bengal. But his early plays show an influence of Samuel Beckett and Harold Pinter.

His play *Evam Indrajit* deals with the existential dilemma of a non-conformist urban middle class youth of the 60s who is ultimately forced to compromise with traditional morality. Indrajit is a rebel for he finds it difficult to adapt himself to the prevalent mores that determine the limits of the existence of his fellow beings. But ironically, he ends up as a conformist to lead placid life like the other youth in the 60s.

Baki Itihas, Sircar's second major play after *Evam Indrajit*, dramatizes the perplexity and bewilderment of some middle-aged intellectuals who failed to do anything useful to the less fortunate ones. In *Bhoma*, Sircar deals with the life in the rural Bengal. Here, the unpardonable urban bourgeois indifference towards the impoverishment of the villagers is realistically dramatized.

A look at the major concerns of these playwrights shows that they have been carried away in the beginning by the themes of topical interest. But they are preoccupied with the common man and social problems as they grow into mature artists.

Undoubtedly, the contemporary dramatist, like his counterpart in any form of literature, aware of the phony values and ever-growing unrest among the youth and exploitation of the poor and needy, responds accordingly. In fact, he feels that as a writer he must speak for the people and he must voice their despair, their longings, their secret shams.[22]

Nevertheless, this initial enthusiasm and commitment begins to lose its vitality, as the writer learns to play the market in search of more lucrative positions in the society. As a matter of fact, such non-conformist attitude of the writer may be a pretext to get into the establishment and his seeming revolt is for selfish motives.[23]

Besides, the creative genius of the writer tends to be marred as he takes a fancy to the worldly pleasures. It is evident from Rajinder Paul's excellent analysis of modern Indian theatre upto the 70s.

> To take the playwrights first. They became conscious of their new status and got carried away by their popularity. Seminars, discussions, the media lap-up and the social circuit, the visible rewards of popularity, left little time for the activity which brought those perks in the first place. The initial burst of creativity was followed by a slow decline in output. . . . By the late 70s . . . Sircar changed course. From an urban playwright he became a proponent of Environmental Theatre. . . . The talents of Karnad and Tendulkar were absorbed by the parallel cinema. Film scripts were a more paying proposition than plays, brought more fame. (42)

Thus, a great change is also perceptible in the writers' outlook on life and literature due to the growing importance of political affairs in the people's life. And it is against this background of changing literary and political values that the plays of Mahasweta Devi are to be viewed.

II

Mahasweta Devi is one of those rare writers who always aspire to find and explore something challenging and new and never accept the existing ideals. Established as a leading novelist with the publication of *Aranyer Adhikar* (The Rights over the Forest) in 1977, Mahasweta Devi has effected a new trend of writing in the Bengali language. The major part of her creative writing is characterized by an unflinching commitment and passion for the underdog.

Born into a well-known artistic family in January, 1926, in Dhaka, Mahasweta Devi grew up at a time when the national movement was at its height. She graduated from Shantiniketan, the 'brain child' of the bourgeois poet, Rabindranath Tagore. Even as a student, she took part in the relief work when the horrible famine of 1943 hit Bengal. Thus, she had come into contact with the political and cultural movements in Bengal. In 1947, she married the dramatist Bijan Bhattacharya who wrote the famous play *Nabanna*. She joined the postal department as Upper Division Clerk but lost this job when the new nationalistic government found her guilty of being a communist. She tried her hand at several jobs, including selling soap dyes and exporting monkeys to the United States.

In 1962, she divorced Bijan Bhattacharya and married the writer Asit Gupta. A year later (seventeen years after graduating from college), she received a master's degree in English literature and took up teaching job at a college located in working class area. She taught here until she resigned in 1984 when she received a call to serve the suffering humanity at large. And she creatively involved herself in the society and sought a full revelation in her fiction of what she found in the world around her. Initially, she contributed stirring articles dealing with problems of common man to the Bengali dailies like *Jugantar*.

As a writer with a social purpose, she stole the scene only after she was given the most coveted Sahitya Akademi award for her novel *Aranyer Adhikar* in 1979 and equally prestigious title

'Padmasree' by the Indian government for her social work in the tribal areas of the three neighbouring states of West Bengal, Bihar and Orissa, especially in the districts of Medinipur, Purulia, Singhbhum and Mayurbhanj.

Having been motivated by a sense of history, her writings hold a mirror to the present and the past. In fact, she was a witness to several people's movements before she became a writer. She says:

> Once I became a professional writer, I felt increasingly that a writer should document his own time and history. The social-economic history of human development has always fascinated me. But some of the greatest political happenings of my times like Tebhaga revolt of the Bengal peasants or the Partition and its aftermath had passed me by before I had become a writer. So I chose to resurrect older periods in history in their immediate physicality, as if they were nothing less than contemporary.[24]

And the major event that occurred after she had become a professional writer, in the late sixties and early seventies, was the Naxalite uprising which seemed to have exerted a tremendous influence on her writings. Surprisingly, unlike the other peasant movements which were led almost by middle-class leadership from Calcutta, this movement sparked off in the Naxalbari area, was led by the unexpected coalition of the peasant and the intellectual. The target of these movements was the long-established oppression of the landless peasantry and itinerant farm worker, sustained through an unofficial government-landlord collusion that too easily circumvented the law.[25] It is no wonder that the event brought about a sea-change in the outlook of the men of letters. Mahasweta Devi is of the opinion that this movement gave rise to a new literary tradition and the writers, artists and cultural activists realized that there was a need to work with the revolutionary to make the people politically aware and lead them to class struggle.[26]

Inspired by the historical events, Mahasweta Devi has written innumerable stories depicting the factors that led to the rebellion and the casualties due to the brutal suppression of the movement.

In her introduction to *Agnigarbha*, a collection of her long stories, all related to the great Naxalite uprising, Mahasweta writes:

> The economic gains that the country has achieved since Independence have not benefitted the middle classes, the workers and the agricultural labourers. The rich have become richer, a brutally complacent and ignorant richer class has come into being . . . those who possessed small plots of land have been compelled to give up their last scraps to the jotedars and moneylenders . . . while nobody heeds to their claims to the right to survive, the hirelings of the affluent middle class and the idle rich weave narcissistic fantasies in the name of literature.[27]

Her acquaintance and involvement with so many different organizations bring her face to face with varied life styles and problems of different communities. She uses her experience to great effect in her writing. Her stories depict the life and situation of people living beyond the limits of the metropolis of Calcutta. As Samik Bandyopadhyay points out, her "plays and stories are often located in communities of the fringe, outside the dominant upper-caste milieu."[28]

A distinctive change is discernible in the writings of Mahasweta Devi from her early years with that of her contemporary writing. Earlier, she wrote in the popular romantic style which appealed, in the main, to the middle class conscience. Besides, she engaged herself in the reconstruction of the past. As Gayatri Chakraborty Spivak justly states, "Mahasweta Devi's own relationship to historical discourse seems clear. She has always been gripped by the individual in history."[29] Her *Amrita Sanchay* (1979), *Andharmanik* (1987) and *Aranyer Adhikar* (1979) are all histories "imagined into fiction." She has done a great deal of research on the subjects on which she wrote. She tells in an article how she undertook an extensive research before she wrote her first historical novel, *Jhansir Ranee* (The Rani of the Jhansi) in 1956:

> Reading the available books and reports in English was not enough. . . . I also read contemporary accounts and lives of

> the Ranee in Bengali, Hindi, Bundelkhandi and Marathi. Then I left for Jhansi . . . at Jhansi I collected the old . . . ballads and met the grass sellers . . . peasants and forest workers. . . . I went to Gwalior where Ranee fell in battle.[30]

According to Mahasweta Devi, "the history of the past and the history of the present . . . constitute history. . . . But there are some histories that are for all times."[31] The history of exploitation of the innocent is a fascinating subject for the Indian creative writers. Mahasweta Devi, having found the enormous spread of exploitative mechanism which is bent on plundering the humanity, is preoccupied with the documentation of the present times.

She thinks that "a responsible writer, standing at a turning point in history, has to take a stand in defence of the exploited. Otherwise history would never forgive him."[31] As such, in the bulk of her creative work, she realistically depicts the untold agonies endured by the rural and urban fringe groups.

There are many forces at work in furthering her identification with the common man. Her father's training and her life experiences have also contributed towards creating a materialist outlook which is evident in her writing. The writings of her great predecessors like Tagore and Sarat Chandra have failed to inspire her. But she expresses her gratitude to Kavi Kankan Mukundaram Chakraborthy (the 16th century poet of Bengal) who gave her an insight into the life of the common man. And his work *Chandika Panahali* remains a source of inspiration even now. She writes:

> Mukundaram awakened my interest in the common people who later became a part of my life. Now I can write about the tribals from first-hand knowledge. That the tribal world remains unexplored is a loss to literature.[33]

Thus, she writes about the everyday life and problems of tribal folk. However, she is not the first writer in contemporary Bengali literature to make tribal life the subject of her writing. There is a long tradition of such writing as is evident from the work of famous writers such as Tarashankar Bandyopadhyay, and Satinath Bhaduri. But there is a remarkable difference in their outlook and that of Mahasweta Devi. In her tribal work, life is not romanticized. Her main concern is to expose the stranglehold of feudalism over land and poor people. So she has "not coloured a single sequence or presented a single falsehood."[34] She has just documented how people live under that oppression. Her sympathetic portrayal aims to capture the pain and torment in the life of the oppressed people. In an interview with Gayatri Chakraborty Spivak, she tells:

> The tribals and the mainstream have always been parallel. . . . The mainstream simply doesn't understand the parallel. . . . They can't keep their land; there is no education for them, no health facilities . . . they are denied everything. . . . That is why I started writing about the tribal movements and the tribal world. . . . I repay them their honor.[35]

As she thinks that innumerable social evils are an off-shoot of the present system, she desires a radical transformation. She writes:

> After thirty-one years of Independence, I find my people still groaning under hunger, landlessness, indebtedness, and bonded labour. . . . All the parties . . . have failed to keep their commitment to the common people. I do not hope to see in my life time any reason to change this conviction of mine. Hence, I go on writing . . . about the people.[36]

Irked by the gross indifference of the contemporary writer towards this suffering humanity, she takes up cudgels against the establishment. She justifies violence where the system fails to do justice. To understand and write about the oppressed life, a creative writer, as she says, "should have a social conscience . . . a duty towards society."[37] And it is unpardonable on the part of the writer who puts on the Nero-like attitude as the people of his country are punished for no fault of theirs. Mahasweta Devi maintains:

> For a long time now, Bengali literature has indulged in a denial of reality and has been plagued by an atrophy of conscience. The writers refuse to see the writing on the wall. The conscientious reader is turning away from them in re-

> vulsion. What can be more surprising than that writers living in a country bedevilled with so many problems . . . should fail to find material for their work in their own country and people?[38]

It is this concern that is also central to her dramatization of her own stories—which appeared time and again in the popular magazines and weeklies like *Desh, Jayashree* and *Basumati* and periodicals like *Prasad.* Thus, her creative work, in spite of "being influenced by a sense of sympathy for the suffering humanity"[39] appears to be stereotyped in terms of content. Mahasweta Devi defends her infatuation with the cause of people who live perpetually below the poverty level. She says:

> I am often asked how long am I to bore my readers with the same themes. My answer is, as long as hunger, poverty, naked exploitation by the rich and the landed, oppression by the government machineries continue, I will continue to write the same things.[40]

Mahasweta Devi is an activist as well as a writer, and even as a writer she is an activist. Since she believes that mere sympathizing with the poor doesn't help, she lives with them in order to bring their grievances and demands to the view of a generally indifferent bureaucracy and set off movements for the redress of different modes of exploitation. So the subjects of her stories become the subjects of her life. In fact, the main thrust in the bulk of her creative work is the release of human soul from all kinds of oppression.

III

Apparently, Mahasweta Devi cares little for the so-called dictum of 'art for art's sake.' What she aims at here is to take message nearer the people in a form that suits the demand and which the people are familiar with. As a result, she dramatizes her own novels and short stories which are translated into English. Surprisingly, play-writing is not her forte. But she chooses this medium as she believes that plays can reach the large illiterate audience. She invests them with the folklore and oral myths which the people's consciousness is steeped in and responsive to. And whatever little criticism is available on her fiction—novels and short stories—can also be applied to her dramatic work.

In fact, Mahasweta Devi, having made an avowal of her sympathies for the exploited, expects less unbiased attention from the contemporary critics. The critical articles surveying the creative work in Bengali and indeed most of Indian languages seem to have been engaged in the promotion of a stock-in-trade type of literature. The creative talent of many a writer has been ignored by this seeming aversion of the critics. The creative work of Mahasweta Devi as a 'cultural exhibit' would not have seen the light, had Gayatri Chakraborty Spivak not presented a 'constructive critique' on her shorter fiction.

Spivak has offered an invaluable criticism in the form of forewords and prefaces to her translations of Mahasweta Devi's 'terrible' stories such as 'Draupadi,' 'Stanadayini' (Breast Giver), 'Douloti' and 'Pterodectyle.' Undoubtedly, the subjugation of women and consequent revolt, a prominent feature of Mahasweta Devi's fiction, gives scope for viewing her work from the feminist point. However, Spivak assigns a subaltern status to Mahasweta Devi for she like a subaltern is scrupulous in her consideration towards women and records moments when men and women are joined in struggle "when their condition of work or education suffer from gender or class discrimination."[41]

Fascinated by the 'history makers,' Mahasweta Devi takes up issues of historical importance and interprets them in a contemporary setting. And the fiction of this sort, observes Spivak, relies for its effect on its 'effect of real': "The plausibility of Jashoda (Stanadayini), a Draupadi (Draupadi, *Agnigarbha*), a Birsa Munda (*Aranyer Adhikar*) is that they could have existed as subalterns in a specific historical moment imagined and tested by orthodox assumptions."[42] These 'shadowy named' characters have plausible being when the subalternist historian imagines a historical moment supported by some counter insurgent or revolutionary feminist textual material. In fact. "the subaltern as object is supposed to be imagined in one case and is real in another" and Mahasweta Devi acknowledges this by claiming to do research.[43]

However, regarding the gendered politics, Colin Mac Cabe's comment appears to be closer to the heart of the matter, when he says: "The force of Mahasweta Devi's text resides in its grounding in the gendered subaltern's body, in that female body which is never questioned and only exploited. The bodies of Jashoda and Dopdi figure forth the unutterable ugliness and cruelty which cooks in Third World kitchen to produce the First World feast that we daily enjoy."[44]

Though Mahasweta Devi quite often refuses to have any affiliation to the politics of the Right or the Left, her writings have been a product of her direct confrontation with the prevailing social norms. And many attempts have been made to infer the influence of Marxist ideology from her creative work. According to Susie Tharu and K. Lalitha, throughout Mahasweta Devi's varied fiction: "Women's subjugation is portrayed as linked to the oppressions of caste and class. But in the best of her writing she quite brilliantly, and with resonance, explores the articulation of class, caste and gender in the specific situations she depicts."[45]

Besides, the protagonists of her stories take to violence when they realize the futility of their protests against repressive social system. As a matter of fact, Mahasweta Devi suggests that violence is necessary to quicken the process of social transformation. Talking about the various manifestations of violence in modern literature, G.N. Devy points out that in Mahasweta Devi's fiction violence is given a Marxist interpretation and all her characters, generally coming from rural backgrounds, are farm workers, tribals, poor women and subalterns. As he observes further: "They face exploitation at the hands of the landlords, Government officials, policemen, money lenders. Almost invariably her protagonists turn violent towards the end of her stories. Theirs is the progressive kind of violence."[46]

Moreover, Mahasweta Devi, as Samik Bandyopadhyay states in his introduction to her *Five Plays*, "throws up leaders of men, moulded, groomed, trained and matured by a whole community, through and within its experience of suffering." (x) All her characters, allowed "to evolve through their interactions with a historical process" (x) are products of exploitation, direct and inhuman.

Therefore, it is no wonder that in all her stories runs a single thread—"a profound concern for the human predicament and sincere hope for the better future of mankind." Thus, taking "every aspect of human suffering to the heart," she focusses on the social evils and "tries to find solutions to problems."[47]

It is evident from the diverse critical opinions that Mahasweta Devi's fiction—historical and domestic—has been instrumental in articulating the agonies of "the dispossessed" and "the disinherited." Though she appears to have been preoccupied with the problem of women, she never views women-folk as a separate entity. In fact, woman is perceived as just another victim, undistinguished from the proletariat in general. Replying to a question—In what ways is the feminist movement relevant to the Indian women?—she admits having no relations with it.[48] Therefore, conferring the title 'feminist writer' on Mahasweta Devi cannot be justified for, according to Janet Todd, "if a feminist is one who is aware of female problems and is angry or mildly irritated at the female predicament, then almost every woman writer and many men could claim the title."[49]

Mahasweta Devi, however, is blissfully unaware of the criticism done on her writings and continues exploring the consciousness of the oppressed 'men' who she identifies herself with, and works for. Thus, she has not felt much of challenge when she, for the first time, transforms her stories into what can be justly termed as 'dramatized documents.'

It is, indeed, strange that there has not been any attempt to evaluate Mahasweta Devi's dramatic achievement and critically place her in the history of the drama in India. It is in her plays that she addresses herself to discovering a suitable medium for her exposition of an accurate profile of contemporary times marked by profound convulsions in individual and collective consciousness. Her plays represent an expression of her deepest concern about the retrograde conventionalities of the modern society. A keen awareness to the happenings around is one of her strong points and she exhibits a deep interest in all matters concerning that section of society which has been ignored by the mainstream Indian life.

Mahasweta Devi, in the main, is a committed dramatist. Her dramatic work stands poles apart from that of the contemporary dramatists for it documents authentically the spirit and passions of the time without any touch of sentimental romanticism. And in the light of this understanding, Mahasweta Devi's plays have been evaluated.

Mahasweta Devi's five plays—*Mother of 1084, Aajir, Urvashi O Johnny, Bayen* and *Water*—are translated and brought out in the form of anthology entitled *Five Plays* by Samik Bandyopadhyay. Besides, she has to her credit many novels and short stories which earned her the reputation of a progressive writer.

The first play in the anthology, *Mother of 1084*, is a moving story of an apolitical mother. The protagonist, Sujata, has been a witness to the horrifying situation during the suppression of the Naxalite uprising in which her own son, Brati, the corpse number 1084, takes part and becomes a martyr. Unable to free herself from the clutches of male dominated society, Sujata fails to realize her own being. But after her discovery of Brati through the confrontation with people outside her respectable existence, Sujata does not remain a passive sufferer. She feels punished for not knowing her son, Brati. She decides to carry out what he left unfulfilled. So, in the end, she exhorts the audience to be active and revolt against the establishment that aims at reducing the young rebels to the level of a mere number which is given to the dead only to be identified by their mothers.

In *Aajir*, Mahasweta Devi deals with the decadent social values and their effects on the illiterate people in the rural areas. Paatan, the protagonist in the play, is a descendant of a family of slaves. His ancestor, Golak, had sold himself and his progeny to perpetual slavery for three rupees. Ignorant of the fact that the bond signed by Golak had long turned to dust, Paatan suffers all sorts of indignities and humiliations at the hands of his master. He is denied the right to a happy life. His cravings for freedom are mercilessly suppressed. The mistress of his landlord, to satisfy her sexual thirst, lets Paatan know about the invalidity of the bond. But he gets to know of the reality of his freedom only after killing the mistress.

Urvashi O Johnny, Mahasweta Devi's play for the Emergency, tells about the love affair of Johnny with Urvashi, a talking doll. Brought up in the slums, he craves for happiness. Hence, he runs away from the orphanage. He learns to play with a talking-doll and gives performances to amuse the people with his tricks. As time passes, Johnny develops cancer in the throat which stands for the suppression of democratic rights during the Emergency. The love affair between Johnny and Urvashi comes to an end when the former collapses on the stage during his last show.

Bayen, the fourth play, presents a powerful tale of harsh reality of a woman's life in rural India. Chandidasi Gangadasi, the protagonist, is put against a powerful exploitative mechanism that is in force in the rural world. She is a professional gravedigger. She buries the dead children and guards them at night. She carries on with her work to please the souls of her forefathers. As she is engaged in the humanitarian work, Chandi is branded as a witch by the superstitious people and separated from her son and family. However much she is relegated to the level of beast, Chandi is still a human being. She exhibits the essential qualities as she dies averting a train accident which would otherwise have resulted in great death toll. In the end, her son, Bhagirath, defies the tradition by acknowledging the witch as his mother.

The play *Water* tells the story of a professional water-diviner, Maghai Dome. He is an untouchable by caste and all the untouchables of the village are forbidden to draw water from the public wells which, in fact, are dug with the help of Maghai's knowledge of water-divining. Santosh Pujari, the villain of the piece, trading in the relief fund meant for the poor, subjects Maghai and his men to untold tortures by denying what is due to them. But towards the end of the play, Maghai, enlightened by Jiten, a school teacher, defies the traditional norms by constructing a dam across the river in order to quench the thirst of his people. But Santosh, having realized a threat to his existence, turns the authorities against them. As a result, there is a confrontation between the oppressor and the oppressed leading to the death of Maghai, the leader of the masses.

The anthology of five plays is a significant exploration of the impact of the constricting conventionalities on the working class people living in both urban and rural Bengal. The protagonist Sujata, Paatan, Johnny, Chandi and Maghai are victims of the repressive social system which cashes in on the gullibility of the weak and the poor. Mahasweta Devi seeks to show how these five sensitive individuals grow into hardcore insurgents by breaking down all the boundaries which are devised by the vested interests to strip the former of its right to live a life of an equal human being. Although at the outset they seem to be conforming to the existing values, they march ahead with an indomitable will of the rebel and embrace martyrdom in the pursuit of their identity which forms the core of her entire dramatic creation.

The present study undertakes to examine Mahasweta Devi's plays, laying stress on their artistic excellence and theatrical vitality. The book is divided into seven chapters. The first chapter makes a survey of the Indian drama in English with a special reference to the major contemporary dramatists—Asif Currimbhoy. Vijay Tendulkar, Girish Karnad and it also posits the place of Mahasweta Devi as an emerging Indian voice in the much neglected field of literature.

The second chapter deals with *Mother of 1084* in which Mahasweta Devi documents the traumatic experiences in the life of a sensitive mother, Sujata, who loses her favourite son in the holocaust during the suppression of the people's movement. Exactly two years after the brutal killing of her son, she becomes not only aware of the need for a sacrifice to defend one's right to live but also her inner urge to protest against the patriarchal authority represented by her husband.

The third chapter is devoted to the play *Aajir* which is a poignant tale of a slave, Paatan, who unlike his forefathers, craves for freedom. Though for a while he follows the tradition, he moves ahead to achieve the cherished goal and kills the mistress of the house.

The fourth chapter is concerned with *Urvashi O Johnny*. Here the playwright explores in depth the realities in the life lived on the pavements of the so-called developed city of Calcutta by making the beggar, who is a ventriloquist by profession, the central figure of the play.

The fifth chapter deals with *Bayen* which tells again a moving story of an innocent mother who, branded as a witch, has been separated from her son and family. She gets killed by averting a train accident which would otherwise have proved fatal. However. in the end, her son defies age-old feudal values by acknowledging the witch as his mother.

The sixth chapter deals with the last play *Water* in which Mahasweta Devi attempts to show how the rural folk, being ignorant of the ways of the world are subjected to exploitation and oppression. Through the leitmotif of 'water,' the transformation of Maghai, an untouchable by caste, takes place from the traditionally defined class role to the position of a leader of the masses.

The conclusion part, apart from summing up the plays discussed in detail in the foregoing chapters, assesses Mahasweta Devi as a dramatist with a social purpose.

NOTES

1. K.R. Srinivasa Iyengar, *Indian Writing in English* (New Delhi: Sterling, 1984), p. 226.
2. M.K. Naik. "The Achievement of Indian English Drama," *The Dimensions of Indian English Literature* (New Delhi: Sterling, 1984), p. 151.
3. *Ibid.*
4. Iyengar, *Indian Writing in English*, p. 236.
5. M.N. Sundararaman, "Tradition and Modernity in Indian English Drama," *Journal of Indian Writing in English*, Vol. 20, no. 1 & 2 (Jan.-July 1992), p. 3.
6. Iyengar, p. 234.
7. S.K. Bhatta, *Indian English Drama: A Critical Study* (New Delhi: Sterling, 1987), p. 30.
8. Indranth Choudhury, "Indianness in Indian Literature," *Comparative Indian Literature: Some Perspectives* (New Delhi: Sterling, 1992), p. 35.
9. M.K. Naik, *A History of Indian Literature* (New Delhi: Sahitya Akademi, 1982), p. 98.
10. Margaret Chatterjee, "Social and Political ideas in Nineteenth and Twentieth Century Bengali Literature," *Indian Literature,* ed. Arabinda Poddar (Simla: Indian Institute of Advanced Study, 1992), p. 269.
11. K.A. Abbas, "Social Realism and Change," *Aspects of Indian Literature: A Changing Pattern*, ed. Suresh Kohli (Delhi: Vikas, 1975), p. 149.

12. Pritish Nandy, "Literature of Protest," *Aspects of Indian Literature*, ed. Suresh Kohli (Delhi: Vikas, 1975), p. 87.
13. Sarit Kumar Bandyopadhyay, "Trends in Modern Bengali Drama," *Indian Writing Today*, Vol. IV (July-Sept., 1970), pp. 149-50.
14. Som Benegal qtd. in Faily Richmond, "The Social Role of Theatre in India," *Marxist Influence and South Asian Literature*, ed. Carlo Coppola (Delhi: Chanakya, 1988), p. 392.
15. Prabhakar Machwe, "Drama: A Search for Modern Idiom," *Four Decades of Indian Literature:A Critical Evaluation*, ed. Machwe (New Delhi: Chaitanya, 1976), p. 130.
16. Samik Bandyopadhyay, introduction, *Five Plays*, by Mahasweta Devi (Calcutta: Seagull Books, 1986), p. xvii.
17. Machwe, p. 137.
18. Naik, *History of Indian Literature*, p. 258.
19. Rajinder Paul, "Modern Indian Theatre," *Seminar*, 359 (July 1989), p. 41.
20. *Ibid.*
21. Veena Noble Dass, "Avant-garde Marathi Playwright: Vijay Tendulkar," *Modern Indian Drama in English Translation* (Hyderabad: Taurus Printers, 1988), p. 91.
22. Pritish Nandy, "Literature of Protest," *Aspects of Indian Literature*, ed. Kohli (Delhi: Vikas, 1975), p. 7.
23. Suresh Kohli, ed., *Aspects of Indian Literature* (Delhi: Vikas, 1975), p. 7.
24. Mahasweta Devi, qtd. Samik Bandyopadhyay, introduction, *Five Plays* (Calcutta: Seagull Books, 1986), pp. vii-viii.
25. Gayatri Chakraborty Spivak, foreword, *Writing and Sexual Difference*, ed Elizabeth Alse (Great Britain: Harvest Press, 1982), p. 265.
26. Mahasweta Devi, "Terai Udyamam," *Srijana* (Telugu), (15 Dec. 1992), p. 19.
27. Qtd. Introduction, *Five Plays*, p. viii.
28. Samik Bandyopadhyay, Afterword, *Five Plays*, p. 167.
29. Gayatri Chakraborty Spivak, "A Literary Representation of the Subaltern: Mahasweta Devi's 'Stanadayini,'" *Subaltern Studies*, V, ed. Ranjit Guha (New Delhi: Oxford University Press, 1987), p. 95.
30. Mahasweta Devi, "Untappped Resources," *Seminar*, 359 (July 1989), p. 15.
31. Qtd. Introduction, *Five Plays*, p. ix.
32. *Ibid.*
33. Mahasweta Devi, "Untapped Resources," *Seminar*, p. 16.

34. Mahasweta Devi, Foreword, *Rakasi Kora* (Trans. into Telugu from the Bengali by S. Sitaram) (Hyderabad Book Trust, 1982).
35. G.C. Spivak, "Notes for Anveshi/Subaltern Studies Conference" (Shelved at Anveshi Research Centre for Women, Hyderabad), pp. 3-4.
36. Qtd. Introduction, *Five Plays*, p. ix.
37. Spivak, "Notes," p. 7.
38. Mahasweta Devi, Preface, *Bashai Tudu,* trans. Samik Bandyopadhyaya, G.C. Spivak (Calcutta: Thema, 1990), pp. xvii-xviii.
39. E. Satyanarayana, "The Unconquered: A Study of Mahasweta Devi's Short Story 'Draupadi,'" *Indian Women Novelists*, ed. R.K. Dhawan.
40. Mahasweta Devi, Foreword, *Rakasi Kora*.
41. G.C. Spivak "Deconstructing Historiography," *In Other Worlds: Essays in Cultural Poliltcs* (New York and London: Methuen, 1987), p. 215.
42. G.C. Spivak, "A Literary Representation of Subaltern: Mahasweta Devi's 'Stanadayini,'" p. 95.
43. *Ibid*, pp. 95-96.
44. Colin Mac Cabe, foreword, *In Other Worlds*, by Spivak, p. xvi.
45. Susie Tharu and K. Lalitha, *Women Writing in India* (New York: The Feminist Press, 1993), vol. II, p. 235.
46. G.N. Devy, "Confrontations with Society," *The Hindu*, August 1, 1993, p. xii.
47. N. Venugopal, "In Wright Earnest," *Indian Express*, 13 October, 1991, p. 2.
48. Interview, "Girijanula Rajakeeya Chaitanyam Nunche Udyamalu Udbavistai," *Praja Paksha Patrika* (Telugu), Sept. 16, 1992, pp. 14-15 (my translation).
49. Janet Todd, qtd. K.K. Ruthven, *Feminst Literary Studies: An Introduction* (Cambridge University Press, 1984), p. 34.

Mother of 1084
Mothers and Rebels

Mahasweta Devi's *Mother of 1084* appeared in Bengali as *Hazar Churashi Ki Ma,* a novel, in the special autumn festival issue of the periodical, *Prasad,* in 1973. Later, it was translated into several Indian languages. She dramatized the novel in 1972-73 when Asit Bose was planning to stage it. Surprisingly indeed, her script has never been staged, though there have been productions of several safe and neutral dramatizations of the novel itself, most of them in Hindi. But, according to Samik Bandyopadhyay, the productions have actually represented the Establishment's endeavour to absorb the exposure with which Mahasweta Devi's novel and play challenged them. The play lends itself to the commercial distortions, even though its naturalistic method gave it a dimension that was beyond the reach of the experimental theatre committed to social comment.[1]

Set in the urban Bengal, the play realistically portrays the climactic phase of the annihilation of the leaders of the masses and its aftermath during 1970s. Keeping out of view the economic and social exploitation in rural Bengal that had drawn landless peasants and tribals to the Naxalite movement, a process which she explores in depth in her work written soon after *Mother of 1084*, especially in *Agnigarbha, Chotti Munda O Tar Teer* and *Sri Sri Ganesh Mahima*, Mahasweta Devi here "concentrates on the reactions of a cross section of survivors, both those who bear the scars and wounds of those horrible days, and those who had lived through the days of violence in simulated insularity." (xi)

Unlike Asif Currimbhoy's *Inquilab* which is a telling commentary on the historical movement that shook West Bengal during 1970s, her play aims to give an artistic expression to the indescribable agonies of sensitive mothers who have been forced to part with their beloved sons.

Mahasweta Devi herself makes the passage from writing historic and domestic fiction to depicting the life-like situations in the contemporary society. As Sujit Mukherjee rightly states, Mahasweta Devi turns, with *Mother of 1084* "to recording the present instead of reconstructing the past."[2] It is a typical play of documentation in which she seeks the roots of the "revolutionary fervour" of the urban rebels "in their discontent with a system that upheld a corrupt and insensitive establishment both in the family and in the State."[3]

In the play, Mahasweta Devi actually deals with an immediate past event in order to comment on the present as a cautionary tale universalizing human experience—an experience which drove many a mother and son to martyrdom.

Though the play, at one level, reads like a mere account of the inhuman suppression of the Naxalite revolt in Bengal, it is a tragedy of an "apolitical" mother who awakens one day to a greater truth and dies a martyr. The realistic surface details such as the mass killing of the young activists, the torture scene and the elaborate party scene are provided only to enable us to penetrate that surface to the hidden truth beneath.

The play enacts a single day in the life of the principal character. Sujata, the mother of corpse number 1084, hails from a fairly affluent middle class family. Though she is a sensitive wife and a loving mother, she is a stranger in her own household where she is reduced to a mere cog. On the contrary, she feels at home in the company of her younger son, Brati Chatterjee, who, unlike her other children, is a man of ideals. And it is his life and activities that Sujata fails to understand which add to the tragic interest of the play.

Exactly two years after the death of her favourite son, Brati, coinciding with his birthday, Sujata gets to know of the facts behind his sacrifice. The learning process continues till the end of the play involving her in a series of encounters with the people whose cause Brati championed.

At the end of the play Sujata, shorn of all prejudices, finds herself drifting towards a kinship with her son's ideology as she bursts out angrily at the lassitude of the audience.

Divided into twelve scenes, *Mother of 1084* is a neatly structured play with a beginning, middle and an end. The identification of the corpse number 1084 forms beginning of the play. Sujata's discovery of Brati constitutes the middle of the play. And her passionate appeal to the people forms the ending of the play.

Mahasweta Devi moves the time-scale backward and forward by presenting the past and the present in alternating scenes, very much in the manner of a memory play. The stage is free of superfluous theatrical properties which give the playwright great freedom to present different situations more by suggestion than by scenic displays without taxing more the belief of the audience. Furthermore, it allows her to be more faithful in her portrayal of the contemporary realities. The shift in the scene is suggested by darkening the stage partly. Besides, the playwright uses the "tape" to great advantage. The "tape" as a device, not only assures the smooth flow of the action in the play but also provides an alternative to rather clumsy dramatic device of soliloquy which is often resorted to by the playwrights to acquaint the audience with what is going on in the character's mind.

The most dominant character in the play is Sujata Chatterjee. She is one of those victims whose kith and kin had been done away with in a confrontation with the people in power. In fact, with Sujata, the playwright seeks to bring to light the darker areas of life where the persecution of the innocent continues unabated. Having felt alienated from her corrupt household, Sujata takes up a job in the bank. Although it is two long years since Brati was killed, her mind is filled with his memories. Not unusually, at times, Sujata tries to find a fulfilment in his death which she has never dared to claim for herself.

Brati, the younger son of Sujata, like other youth, disillusioned with the present social system—a system that harbours many evils which thrive on the gullibility of the innocent people, responds accordingly to the People's Movement sparked off with the peasant revolt in the rural West Bengal and spread to the metropolis when the urban intelligentsia, out of a sense of remorse, decides to take part in it "for their guilt in acquiescing in the perpetuation of a system of exploitation from which they had reaped benefits for generations."[4]

Like Sujata, Brati has no fancy for the luxuries that their rich background is to offer. Being aware of economic deprivation and exploitation, he swears by the cause of the exploited. And he revolts against the senseless ethics of all those institutions that add to the woes of the underdog. It is, however, unexpected of a person like him who is a member of a family which has been built on the mound of corruption which touches the play with a curious mix of the elements of surprise, innocence and youth imminent in life and history.

It is indeed surprising that Sujata, with an innate resentment, like her favourite son, against all the shams that are inherent in the patriarchal institution, fails to take cognizance of the rising tide of revolt in Brati. Thus, Sujata, is caught in the conflict within herself between a sympathetic mother and a silent protester against the immoral life which her household stands for.

This conflict assumes an altogether different form when her motherly love is contrasted with the indifference of the members of her family towards the news of Brati's death with which the play begins.

Dibyanath Chatterjee, the husband of Sujata, is an overbearing and complacent man. He does not hesitate to risk the private sentiments to keep his public stature untarnished. He knows how to play the cards properly to improve his domain on the established lines. This attitude of his is vividly depicted in the opening scene of the play when they receive a phone-call from the police to identify corpse number 1084 which is, in fact, Brati's. While Sujata is all concerned and helpless, Dibyanath searches for the ways to hush up the incident. The following opening dialogue illustrates this:

The impersonal voice of an officer (off): 460001?
Sujata: Yes.
Voice: Dibyanath Chatterjee's house?
Sujata: Yes. . . .
Voice: Is there no male member around?
Sujata: Still sleeping. Who are you?
Voice: What's Brati's relationship with you?
Sujata: Son.

Voice: Son? Come to Kantapukur. . . . you have to identify Brati. . . .

Dibyanath: What's the matter? Who was it? . . .

Sujata: He said, Come to Kantapukur . . . to identify? Brati?

Dibyanath and Jyoti look at each other, with a clear understanding of what has happened.

Dibyanath: Kantapukur?

Sujata: Haven't I told you? Jyoti, get me the car out. . . .

Dibyanath: My car, at Kantapukur? No. Listen Jyoti. . . .

Sujata: But why? Why can't the car be there?

Dibyanath: I need the car. I'm going to Chaudhari. You, ring up Dutta. Tell him . . . why don't you go over straightaway? . . . Jyoti, there may be time still. Isn't there a relation of your mother-in-law's in the police? . . . Ring him up. Chaudhari must help hush it up. (4-5)

The indifference shown by Dibyanath and his children is the most characteristic of a section of the people that passes for the elite which indulges in self-care and self-love. The mask of detachment they put on is only a pretext to cover up their misdeeds and escape punishment.

Mother of 1084 satisfies every requirement of a successful first scene. As C.V. Venugopal observes: "A playwright invariably has to be very careful with his first scene if he is to be assured of a satisfactory impression on the audience."[5] Thus, as a well-written exposition, the first scene of the play not only suggests the central conflict but also convincingly introduces the major characters—Sujata, Brati and Dibyanath.

In fact, one important feature of the play is that it sets off with characters not already formed but emerging from the play. As such, all the characters, except Sujata Chatterjee, are given minor portions in the play. Even Brati, around whom the entire story of the play is woven, is allotted only a few dialogues and he appears in the beginning as corpse number 1084. As a living character we find him only twice—in the company of his mother (Scene 5) and with his friends (Scene 7). However, Brati and his activities are revealed to us when the principal character Sujata gets herself engaged in conversation with different characters at different places which marks the progress of the play.

Irony permeates *Mother of 1084*. Sujata feels suffocated under the weight of the stifling values enjoined on her by the patriarchal institution. Yet she never ventures to disentagle herself from them. She is aware of her husband's womanizing and corrupt practices, but she says nothing against him. Rather she tries to escape all the constraints by taking up a job in the bank. Though at times she resents the immoral acts of her children, she continues to discharge her familial duties, bearing calmly all kinds of humiliations. She is very fond of her youngest son, Brati who unlike her other children is a man of integrity. She appears to find in his company what she misses in her household. The natural relationship between a mother and her son is excellently evoked when the playwright attempts to create a sentimental situation in Scene 5. Consider the following:

Brati: (pulls his eyes down) Mother, you have to bear with a lot for me, eh?
Sujata: No, Brati, Bear with a lot for you? Oh, no.
Brati: Don't they bully you a lot for me?
Sujata: Let them.
Brati: (with tenderness and concern) Why do you bear, mother?
Sujata: It hurt once, doesn't hurt any longer. It doesn't hurt from the time you came, because you're there.
Brati: Because I'm there!
Sujata: Oh, let it go. You tell me now what you'll have for dinner tomorrow.
Brati: Why? What's special about tomorrow?
Sujata: Don't you remember, it's your birthday. . . .
Brati: How can you remember birthdays?
Sujata: How can I help remembering? I was almost dying when you were born.
Brati: Lucky you didn't? (14)

Ironically, however much they value each other's feelings, Sujata does not know enough about Brati's activities. It is only with the help of others that she learns what he is really made of. As a matter of fact, her first meeting with Nandini, an activist and faithful follower of Brati, provides Sujata with an insight into a part of her son's life that she had never known. And she realizes how he risked his life by staying back home on his birthday to honour her sentiments. "Otherwise," says Nandini, "he should have left . . . for the base on the fifteenth" (25) and escaped death.

Here, in his total commitment to revolution, Brati reminds us of Ahmed of *Inquilab* by Asif Currimbhoy. But unlike Ahmed who mercilessly kills his parents, Brati remains till his death a loyal son of his parents even though he knows about his father's corrupt life. He has a high opinion of his mother, for "he hadn't seen in his life a person as totally honest" (23) as her.

Brati, as an ideal rebel, never makes his true self known to Sujata for he does not want the familial sentiments prevail upon his revolutionary fervour. For him, the mission of life is to emancipate the mankind from the clutches of the hydra-headed exploitative mechanism and create a class-less society where people enjoy equal rights.

But the representatives of the ruling party like Saroj Pal regard the young rebels as a "cancerous growth on the body of Democracy" (9) and view their activities as a threat to the status quo. Hence, there is a conflict—a conflict between the exploiter and the exploited—leading to senseless assaults and counter-assaults and an orgy of violence and murder in the name of fake encounters. Brati, the TEN EIGHTY FOUR is killed along with his friends—Somu, Partha and Bijit, in such an encounter with the goons of the ruling party.

Each visit of Sujata to the people beyond the circuit of her experience is, in a way, a confrontation which opens up the secret areas of understanding. In fact, these confrontations take place across the cleavages of hierarchies of power, of class and commitment.[6] The play is full of such confrontations which serve a two-fold purpose—of letting the protagonist come face to face with the realities of life and of self-realization.

Involved in such situations, Sujata is in conflict with the world around her. Having been compelled to adapt herself to the prevailing social norms and traditions, Sujata has unwittingly become a part of them. They have gone into her consciousness. And, she is not bold enough to bring about a revolution to change them.

As a result, she pays no heed to Brati's revolt against the age-old social values. And what is more surprising is that Sujata has been pathetically ignorant of her fault until Nandini, turning searchlight on her, tells:

Nandini: I loved Brati.
Sujata: I know (pause). It leaves one so empty when you think of it, Nandini. Brati was the soul of my life, yet I know him so little.
Nandini: Did you ever try?
Sujata: Is it a relationship where you have to try?
Nandini: It's a deadly time when people do not belong to one another by virtue of kinship or ties of blood. Everyone remains a stranger these days to every other one. It's a crime to allow this to persist. It's an obligation these days to know one's son.
Sujata: Is it an obligation for parents alone?
Nandini: It's for you to take the first step. Isn't it your obligation to set a model for the younger generation to follow? Why do you demand loyalty by virtue of relationship? Why don't you try to earn it by virtue of your integrity? You won't be honest, won't forge relationships, and then put the whole blame on us. (24)

This is the voice of an angry young woman crippled by the police torture. Her unwavering faith in human dignity is inspiring. It is in her company, Sujata's true self is laid bare. Nandini says: "How can you be so smug and complacent? With so many young men killed, so many imprisoned, how can you wallow in your complacency? It's your "all's right with the world, let's go on nicely" that frightens me most. How can you carry on with your pujas, concerts, cultural festivals, film festivals, poetry fests?" (29-30)

Although the rubble left by the Naxalite storm has been cleared, the memories of the upheaval still haunt the survivors. They could not reorient themselves to the mainstream life. Somu's father is a "timid man all his life, he had never learnt to cheat." (12) Unaware of the enormity of the crime perpetrated by the Establishment with tacit support from the police, he feels cheated. At the outset, he, like others, believed that the government would come to his rescue. He ran to the police for help, when the outrageous mob attacked and killed his son, Somu, along with Brati. But all his hopes of saving them were shattered. Somu's mother says: "they wouldn't even take down his complaint. They didn't do a thing. They only sent their vans when it was all over to collect the dead bodies. . . . They didn't do a thing. That was more than he could bear, and he died of the shock. O God! No justice? He went on and on asking till he was dead." (19)

Having lost thus the last bread-winner in the family, many mothers and sisters have given themselves up to despair. Their social position is pathetic, painful, even heart-rending, as is evident in the complaint made by Somu's mother to Sujata, which reflects the antinomy of life that seems to mock the fate of history of individual lives. However, the reciprocal temptation of grief and hope in that moment heightens the sense of human conflict.[7] Somu's mother tells Sujata:

> My daughter tells me, don't cry. Will he come ever? . . . Think of Partha's mother, sister, she handed her son over to Death. Partha's younger brother can't come back home. They'd kill him too, if he came back. . . . Even now. There're thousands of them, young men, all homeless. All those families banished from the colony. It leaves one sick at heart even to think of them.

She continues further:

> How can there be quiet with the mothers' hearts burning like bodies on fire? . . . It's not easy to . . . feed two souls, mother and daughter. Somu had to leave us behind, all at sea. . . . You have yet another son. You can still hold him to your breast and forget your grief. . . . I lost my son, my son's father and hapless I, with this tortoise's life of mine, shall live on forever, and two funeral pyres burning within! (10-19)

Thus, Sujata goes through a painful process of discovering Brati and her own being while others in the family including Dibyanath, the father, enjoy socializing with those persons who have been overtly a part of the Establishment that cause Brati's death. She is now fully aware of the situation in which she lives. The more she learns about Brati, the closer she feels to him. She can find him among the people who he strove and died for. Though initially, grief had brought them and Sujata together, she finds herself always on the receiving end. Somu's mother tells Sujata:

Somu's mother: Your son, sister, gifted his life away. He had come to warn Somu and his group. They had got wind that the four of them were there in the colony, there was the fear that they wouldn't survive the night. . . .

Sujata: I hadn't ever seen them. (Pause) Brati had never brought them home. (Pause) I wasn't home all the time.

Somu's mother (draws a breath): You're a working woman, you've a rich home, I wonder why Brati chose such a course! Didn't you ever realize what your son was up to? (11-12)

The barriers that separated Sujata from the rest of the people like Somu's mother appear to be dwindling away. She could find an echo of her own silent scream of torment and desperation in their unending sufferings. However, finding in her a rebel in the making, the vested interests do not allow her to visit the settlements of the underdog. The relationship, established between Sujata and Somu's mother—both of them victims of the holocaust during the 1970s—is not unnatural and it possibly turns a major threat to the prevailing social system as the victims learn to make common cause by revolting against all kinds of oppression. Somu's mother asks Sujata not to come again to her house for "They tell her, why does she come to your house? Forbid her. It'll be dangerous otherwise." (20) Talking about the effects of the Naxalite revolt on the life of the common man, Sumanta Banerjee in an article entitled "Sting of Betrayal" rightly states that there are hundreds of victims, "who are not being allowed to lead a normal life. For years the police have been trained to suspect every young man as a potential rebel, and they find ready preys even among those unfortunate youth who were perhaps once on the fringe of the Naxalite movement but have no political connections whatsoever now."[8]

Having realized how she is chained everywhere and how she fails miserably to rid herself of the constraints of the tradition, Sujata says: "I won't go to Somu's mother. I won't come to you [Nandini]. I won't go to the place where Brati exists. Maybe that's my punishment for not knowing Brati." (30)

Motivated by a selfless desire to bring in a "new era," the young men like Brati take to revolutionary activities. They have pledged everything to the cause of all. The temptations of money, job and power do not mean a thing to them. But why does it always fall short of the expectations? Betrayal and "an overdose of romanticism" (22) play an important part in this regard. Nandini tells Sujata: "Why we hadn't provided for the possibility of people joining the party as friends only to betray us ultimately. . . . We didn't have a clue to reality. . . . I still wonder how we could afford not to know that with all that has happened since 1947, all human loyalties had dissolved by 1970. I wonder how we could be unaware that they could betray us to kill us. . . . We could be shocked whenever we heard that behind assassination there was one closely related to the victim." (22)

Besides, the Establishment is all set to eliminate the leaders of the masses, the agents like Anindya, one-time associate of Brati and Saroj Pal, a "bloody cur of the police" (9) carry out its orders in exchange for handsome rewards. Saroj Pal, an archetype of bureaucracy, surpasses all those persecutors who have come to stay in our memory by virtue of their notoriety. The description of the interrogation scene, in which he adopts cruel techniques to elicit information from Nandini, is realistic:

Saroj Pal: What was your relation with Brati Chatterjee? Was he a friend?

Nandini: Stop it.

Saroj Pal: What was your relationship with Brati. . . . (Bends close to her, lights a cigarette, presses the lighted cigarette to Nandini's cheek. She screams.). . . He puffs at cigarette and then presses it again to Nandini's cheek. The questions and the pattern continue. (28)

Consequently, a 'whole generation' of people between 'sixteen and forty' is wiped out. And the survivors of the killed either learn to adjust or revolt. The revelations made by Nandini and Somu's mother are severe indictment of the Establishment's inhuman attitude towards its rebels. Nandini says: "Nothing's changed. Thousands of young men rot in the prisons without trials, they are denied the status of politicals. . . . Torture continues with greater sophistication and secrecy." (29)

As the play progresses we realize the supreme irony of the situation—the men who like Brati, committed to the cause of humanity, are subjected to physical torture and death whereas the turncoats like Anindya go scot-free. And the reward for the mothers like Sujata is only a sophisticated number—"THE TEN EIGHTY FOUR" to identify the corpses of their sons among a thousand other corpses at the official mortuary.

The number '1084' conferred on the corpse of Brati symbolizes at once the countless horrors that gripped the common life during the brutal suppression of the People's Movement in the seventies and the Establishment's endeavour to reduce its insurgents to the level of an insignificant being.

Brati gains in superhuman proportions when compared with the others in the family. For the first time, Sujata realizes the significance of the sacrifice made by Brati and she reacts sharply when her children make flippant remarks by dragging him into their discussion:

Sujata: Brati's belief was so different from your belief in the Swami, or Bini's in her prayer room, that it sounds utterly absurd when you drag his name into the same context.

Tuli: You will react every time we mention Brati. . . . Are we not worthy enough to pronounce his name?

Sujata: The way you pronounce it! To hurt me! . . . To Tony and his crowd, to the others. You, your father, Jyoti, Neepa, the way you all speak his name, as if. . . . Brati was a criminal. (8)

Sujata's identification with Brati is total. For her, Brati is more than a mere son. He represents a whole class of people who staked their lives for the sake of noble values. Though the Establishment dehumanized him by giving a number to his corpse, Brati is still a human being. Sujata feels satisfied when she finds in his revolt a parallel to her suppressed protest against the decaying middle class mores. In fact, Sujata's discovery of Brati and his cause helps her to rediscover her "self" and her cause as a mother, a woman and a human being. And she does not regret being classed with Brati. She recalls: "With Brati, they've cast me too in the opposite camp. If Brati had been like Jyoti, or drunkard like Neepa's husband, Amit or a hardened fraud like Tony, or had run after the typists like his father, he'd have belonged to their camp." (10) Sujata finds herself in direct conflict with a group of hypocrites that is her so-called respectable household which she has so far failed to disconnect herself with. She remains a passive spectator while the guests and her household join the festivities held on the occasion of her daughter's engagement. In fact, it is the day on which Brati was born and also died. And it is the day on which Sujata finds her Brati again: "I was with Brati the whole day." (32)

The rift between Dibyanath and Sujata has widened further when the former accuses her of being responsible for the death of Brati. Baseless though it is, the accusation accelerates her realization of which side she is on ideologically. She seems to have felt relieved of the burden of sinful life she has lived all these years.

But in a society which is full of Dibyanaths and Saroj Pals, she seems to have realized that a greater revolt and higher sacrifice like Brati's is essential to safeguard human values.

She is a working mother for whom her work is in itself a form of protest and self-assertion against the patriarchal authority of her husband. But she cannot help obliging the familial responsibilities. Forced to take part in the festive occasion, Sujata does not feel at ease. Thus, stage is set for the inevitable when Saroj Pal, the DCDD (Deputy Commissioner, Detective Department), a friend of her son, Tony, turns up to convey his best wishes. His presence strikes a chill into her heart. She feels hemmed in on all sides by the enemy. The direction reads: "She grips her throat to stop the scream from breaking forth. There is a stare of disbelief in her eyes." (34) She is reminded of Saroj Pal's cold and business-like attitude on the day she was summoned to the morgue to identify Brati's dead body.

> (Voice on tape, off): I've mother too. No, your son never went to Digha. . . . No, we'll not leave these in the house. . . . What your son did is unforgivable. . . . No, you won't get the body. . . . No, not the body. (34-35)

Having found Saroj Pal "still in uniform . . . still on duty . . . still the Black Maria, the revolver in the holster, the helmeted policemen within the van" she becomes alert for there will be another mass action "in Baranagar and Kashipur today." (35) And the play ends with Sujata exhorting the audience, that is people, not to be silent sufferers, but respond actively to the reality and the cause. She knows it is a common cause in which she has merged her 'self':

> Why don't you speak? Speak, for heaven's sake, speak, speak, speak! How long will you endure it in silence? Where is the place where there's no killer, no bullets, no prison, no vans? . . . Where can you escape it all . . . in Calcutta, in West Bengal, from north to south, from east to west? (35)

Here it is the voice of a universal protest against the seemingly immovable and heartless society in which we live. And, by the time she makes this stirring appeal to the audience, Sujata shakes herself off the shackles of the patriarchal values enjoined on woman. Enlightened, she takes up cudgels against the society itself. Symbolically, Sujata moves from the world of innocence to the world of experience. As a result, she discovers inside herself a wish for self-realization which has been so far suppressed due to the lack of courage.

In fact, her confrontation with Somu's mother and Nandini makes her aware of the seedy side of life which she has been a stranger to. She identifies herself with the cause of the suffering humanity. Particularly, the story of Nandini who, blinded "from the gleam of the thousand watt lamps," (30) is "out on parole. For medical treatment. They wouldn't have let me out otherwise," (30) not only moves Sujata to pathos but also exposes her to the hard realities of the contemporary society. Nandini reveals:

Nandini: Do you think they've stopped only because the newspaper don't report them? Arrest? Torture? Murders in the name of encounters?

Sujata: Don't tell me. (24)

A moment later, we find in Sujata an altogether different mother who appears to be throwing defiance in the teeth of immoral social values. The following passage illustrates this:

Sujata: It's time for me to leave.

Nandini: Yes. It's your youngest daughter's engagement party.

Sujata: I'll come again. . . .

Nandini: No. What do you gain out of coming to me? You live with your past. I have to harness my present, think of the future. . . . Come, let me show you the way.

Sujata: Never mind. I'll find my way out. (30)

It is true that Sujata discovers a new way—a way of realizing her being as mother, which stands her apart but as a model for humanity. It is revealed further in the beginning of the final scene when the playwright uses the recorded tape to convey her inner thoughts: "Brati, I spent the whole of the day with you, and I can't forget myself now to carry out my duties." (31)

Actually, the day-long odyssey into the life lived beyond the circuit of her so-called respectable existence, brings her face to face with the reality of the death of ONE THOUSAND AND EIGHTY FOUR rebels. She finds an image of Brati in every youth who steps unknowingly into the trap laid by the vested interests. She cries out alarmingly: "You can't be on the run any longer, Brati. Brati, come back. I found you back today, Brati. If the siren screeches again, if the vans rush, and Saroj Pal chases another young man somewhere you'll be lost again." (35)

Sujata thinks that the human society, given itself to the pleasures of the modern world, is devoid of human qualities. Hence, the noble sacrifice like that of Brati's is in vain. She asks:

> (Pointing to the audience, and the dancers) Corpses, stiffened corpses, all of you! (Pointing to herself) And I myself? Did

> Brati die to let you carry on in your cadaverous existence, enjoying and indulging in all the images of the world . . . for ever, till infinity? Never. . . . Let this No of mine . . . set the past, the present, and the future ashiver. Let it tear down the happiness of everyone cooped up in his own happy happiness. (35-36)

With this outburst, directed against the pleasure-seeking people, Sujata collapses on the stage. However, her search for Brati does not end with her death. It continues as a problem very much alive.

NOTES

1. Samik Bandyopandhyay, introduction, *Five Plays* by Mahasweta Devi (Calcutta: Seagull Books, 1986), pp. xii-xiii.
2. Sujit Mukherjee "Mahasweta Devi's Writings—An Evaluation." *Book Review*, Vol. XV, No. 3 (May–June, 1991), p. vii.
3. Samik Bandyopadhyay and Gayatri Chakraborty Spivak, introduction, *Bashai Tudu* by Mahasweta Devi (Calcutta: Thema,1990), p. vii.
4. *Ibid.*, p. viii.
5. C.V. Venugopal, "Larins Sahib," *Perspectives on Indian Drama in English,* ed. M.K. Naik and Mokashi-Punekar (Madras: Oxford University Press, 1977), p. 171.
6. Bandyopadhyay and Spivak, Introduction, *Bashai Tudu*, p. viii.
7. E. Satyanarayana, "Mothers in Mahasweta Devi's Plays: *Mother of 1084* and *Bayen*," *Kakatiya Journal of English Studies*, Vol. XIII (1993), p. 140.
8. Sumanta Banerjee, "Sting of Betrayal," *Economic and Political Weekly* (Feb. 5, 1983), p. 176.

Aajir: Dialectics of Human Bondage

Mahasweta Devi's *Aajir*, the second play in the anthology of *Five Plays* appeared as a story before it was adopted into a play during 1976-77. Here in *Aajir*, like in *Mother of 1084*, Mahasweta Devi seeks to expose yet another area of exploitation and oppression. With *Aajir*, she ostensibly moves from the urban world to the rural world where the oppression of the innocent is perpetrated on a larger scale.

While *Mother of 1084* is concerned with the history of 'the present,' *Aajir* deals with an age-old social evil which has reduced the humanity to a sub-human level. In her preface to a recent collection of her stories, Mahasweta Devi comments:

> The history of the past ('Champa,' 'Dewana,' 'Khoimala') and the history of the present ('Shareer,' 'Dheebar,' 'Pindadan,' 'Jawl,' 'Wrong Number'), both constitute history. There are some histories that are for all times ('Aajir,' 'Stanadayini').[1]

Aajir is essentially a social play in which Mahasweta Devi attempts to give an artistic expression to the sufferings of the under-privileged in their confrontation with the powerful exploitative mechanism, which according to Samik Bandyopadhyay,

> operates beyond the law and with the tacit acquiescence of an exploited class held in thrall by a load of conventional role obligations. Legal reforms or legal defences for the exploited have rarely affected the exploitative mechanism sustained by the illiteracy/ignorance of the exploited. (xv)

Aajir, a story of a slave held in slavery by a bond signed by an ancestor, presents a realistic picture of the rural India where the barbaric system of bonded labour has been at work. The bonded labour system, in fact, has its origin in the Varna system. Indian society had been stratified into four Varnas (castes)—Brahmin, Kshatriya, Vaishya and Shudra. The people belonged to the varna of shudra were denied a right to property, education and choice of occupation. They were made to depend on others for their survival. Their total dependence on other caste Hindus reduced their status to that of slaves. Even today, most of the bonded labourers belong to this section of the people. In his important book on *Bonded Labour in India*, N.D. Kamble rightly states: "In practice, bonded labour in India is the culmination of the debtor-creditor relation into slave and master relation. But the bonded labour is an outcome of socio-economic system prevailing in India. Some people who were deprived of the socio-economic and political powers had to depend on those who enjoyed these powers. Criminal poverty of vulnerable sections exposed them to exploitation in the built-in-mechanism of socio-economic system. Economic dependence and poverty of the under-privileged sections of the society forced them to be slaves."[2]

Though, apparently, Mahasweta Devi's *Aajir* is set against this background, her own perception and outlook on the life of the suffering humanity gives the play a new dimension. In her capacity as an active social worker and journalist, Mahasweta Devi has come into contact with the lives and struggles of the under-privileged communities settled in the border regions of the three neighbouring states of West Bengal, Bihar and Orissa. She has been a witness to many a pathetic incident in their lives which has hitherto found no expression in the contemporary writings.

In fact, as she is aware, even after four decades of freedom and enlightenment, India miserably fails to realize what could be called the ideals of Welfare State. Besides, the life beyond the mainstream withers away under the weight of the conventions reminiscent of the dark ages. The innocent people still experience the trauma of inhuman subjugation by the landlords who reign supreme in the villages. In an interview with Gayatri Chakraborty Spivak, Mahasweta Devi reflects:

> In 1965, I started going to Palamu. . . . Palamu is still an inaccessible district, the poorest in the state of Bihar. . . . In such backward, feudally oppressed districts, the bonded labour system survives. The bonded labour system was introduced by the British. They created a new class, which took away tribal land and converted the tribals into debt-bonded slaves . . . from Kashmir to the Indian ocean, and from East to West, in every state . . . there are more than forty thousand bonded laborers in each of them. . . . I have covered all of the (Bihar) district on foot. . . . Thus bonded labour system, in its naked savagery and its bloody exploitation . . . became clear to me.[3]

Drawing the idea for the play "from a slave bond executed by a slave who sold himself into slavery . . . in the family history of the Mustafis of Ulo-Birnagar,"[4] Mahasweta Devi brings to light those darker areas where an individual, being a descendant of a family of slaves, is subjected to unmerited tortures and reduced to the subhuman status—a status that denies him a right to love and marry.

In *Aajir*, Mahasweta Devi creates a character who seeks identity for himself in a world which has for ages suppressed his kind. The protagonist, Paatan, like Bakha in *Untouchable* by Mulk Raj Anand confronts a society that denies him a right to live a life of an equal human being. He is destined to do a work he hates. Unlike his predecessors who sold themselves and their progeny happily into the 'perpetual slavery' for a meagre amount of three rupees, Paatan defies the tradition by yearning for freedom.

However, his attempts to free himself from the clutches of slavery and to lead a life of a respectable human being are foiled. He is subjected to inhuman treatment. The mistress of the house, with a view to get her sensual desires satisfied, pretends to be helping him. Keeping out of him the secret of the bond that has "long turned to dust," she continues to flirt with him. The lure of 'release' from the bondage makes Paatan agree to the mistress's proposal of elopement.

Paatan feels cheated when she tells him that there is no 'bond' which gives her husband a hold on him. He does not believe it.

He pounces on her and kills. In fact, the play ends with the master of the house revealing the fact that he himself is not aware of a thing like 'bond' and Paatan has been a slave and has suffered for no fault of his. Now, he has no regrets and moves to prison raising "his head and stretches his hands out in regal dignity." (58)

Simplicity is the strength of *Aajir*. The play is written in scenes. Each scene is logically connected with the other. The playwright has not employed any technique except for the device of 'tape.' Once the curtain rises, the action of the play moves on smoothly. The play, very much in the manner of folk-theatre, is free of all sorts of theatrical properties. At no place do we find any description of the setting in the form of stage direction. This device is not without purpose.

In fact, the naked stage gives the playwright a greater freedom to present a character in the present enacting a happening in the past. And it also allows her to be more faithful in her dramatization of the realities of the oppressed life without recourse to unnecessary scenic displays. As such, she takes every care to present her subject realistically. Hence, there is no attempt to disguise the stage apparatus. This invariably reminds us of Brecht who, in order to produce a good dramatic effect, employs 'anti-illusionist' theatrical device.[5] Here Mahasweta Devi, like him, tries to establish direct connection between the audience and the actors thereby focussing the attention of the former on the point she is trying to drive home through the latter.

Aajir is essentially a realistic play. It presents an awful and degrading picture of slavery that has been prevalent in the most parts of agricultural West Bengal. It also gives us an opportunity to see how the rural-folk, being illiterate and ignorant, become victims of exploitation and are driven to the eternal servitude.

Paatan, the protagonist in the play, is a bondservant. He is a descendant of a great family of slaves that "lived in the Bengali era 1101, corresponding to 1072 of the Hijra era." (41) But unlike his predecessors who had spent their lives in servitude, Paatan yearns for a free life. He always thinks of escaping into world where there is no MASTER and where he can have a family of his own.

Thus, Paatan is caught in the conflict between a world which despises and degrades him and a will that wages a relentless war against it to keep his identity. However, Paatan, like Sujata Chatterjee in *Mother of 1084*, is a silent protester. He resiliently suffers all sorts of humiliations at the hands of his master, Maatang Shunri. And we do not find any sign of revolt in Paatan till the end of the first scene which, in fact, enacts his ancestor's loathsome selling of himself to slavery.

Before the actual play begins, a voice—probably from an invisible 'Sutradhar'—is heard three times as saying: "The term aajir stands for one who has sold himself to be a slave for a paltry sum." (40) This statement, in fact, serving as an introduction sets going the story. But its repetition highlights the predicament of humanity which has been exploited and marginalized from time immemorial. Paatan introduces himself to the audience:

> I am an aajir (Pause. Then he shouts) Sirs, my dear sirs, I'm an aajir. . . . Ages ago, in the hoary past, there was once a terrible famine in the tracts of our Ayodhya hills. And then. . . . (He breaks into a dance with an imaginary drum, beating it even as he rotates in a circle, singing)
>
> It began with the drought,
> with the crops drying up on the fields,
> and hundreds dying of hunger,
> all the rice and all the grains
> piling up in Raavan Shunri's granary,
> till my forefather Golak Kura,
> to save his life. . . .
>
> (Pauses, then in a wail, in prose) sold himself and his wife Gairabi Dasi away for only three rupees. . . . He sold away all his descendants too at once . . . (39)

It is the tone of a person who, committed in spite of himself to slavery, holds himself upto mockery which gives the play an ironic touch.

Paatan is conscious of his precarious social position. He can not but follow the tradition that had been started by his forefathers. Paatan's ancestor, Golak Kura, born "in a land of famines, nurtured by famines, scared of famines" had doomed his descendants "to the lives of aajirs." (42)

Thus, Paatan has lost his freedom. Even he seems to have lost his human qualities. His is the condition of a bird caught and caged for the pleasure of its master. Here, we are undoubtedly reminded of Harindranath Chattopadhyaya's famous social play *Parrot*, in which a woman character, having been subjected to conventional morality, longs for freedom. She addresses the parrot:

> Poor caged bird!—and he bought you at the market for a rupee—one rupee—and for that one stupid little round coin of silver you have lost your freedom . . . You have lost the sky and the meaning of your wings. . . . You have lost the language of your soul and with it your mate . . . you yearn for freedom? But it is no use.[6]

Though the situation in which the woman is made to utter these words is different from the present, whatever she says here, of the "poor caged bird" is strangely true of Paatan.

Rural folk, in general, have been a victim of an incorrigible exploiter—moneylender. But, particularly in West Bengal, the major part of rural life is dominated by the three men—"Bhuinya the Zamindar, Sau the moneylender, and Barari the Jotedar." Interestingly, it is these three persons who are scared, run a parallel government in the villages. During famines, they not only hoard up the essential commodities creating an artificial scarcity of food, but also misuse the relief funds meant for the poor. Consequently, several of the labour-folk leave their villages for safer places and others, finding no alternative become slaves.

Impoverished thus by both natural and man-induced calamities, the innocent people, in order to get at least a meal a day, are forced to mortgage their property and themselves to the landlord-cum-moneylender for the amount fixed by him. They become indebted for life as they are unable to repay the amount. In fact, the rate of interest is very high and is compounded. As a result, it multiplies more than the principal amount within a year. In her novelette, *Operation? Bashai Tudu*, Mahasweta Devi aptly comments:

> The moneylender's book of accounts is like a python that can

> swallow its prey, but cannot disgorge it. Once a plot of land had got into the book of accounts, there was never a chance of its coming out again. Any kind of land, dry or fertile . . . was like Abhimanyu in the *Mahabharata*, the one knew the way into the destructive formation made by the enemy but did not know how to get out of it, or like food in the maws of a python.[7]

Therefore, it is not surprising, that the hapless, sometimes, when they are left with nothing to avoid the impending death, sell themselves to the landlord who in turn provides for generations "oil for their hair, clothes for their bodies, and rice for their stomachs." (40-41)

The whole process of pauperization and resultant slavery comes to life when Paatan recalls how he became an aajir:

> Watch, gentlemen, how a man becomes a slave from birth. Please allow me to become my forefather, Golak Kura. (He leaps to the centre of the stage, Raavan and his companions surround him and revolve around him)

Golak: (shouting) Is there anybody here ready to buy me? Husband and wife, were here to sell ourselves. (Looking into the wings) Come here, aunt! (Golak's wife comes in and stands. The same actor plays both Golak and Paatan. The same actress acts Golak's wife and Paatan's master's wife. The same actor plays Raavan and Maatang.)

Raavan: You'll sell yourselves?

Golak: Who's there to buy us?

Raavan: I'll buy you.

Golak: That'll be a great relief.

Raavan: I have the bond already written out. The witnesses are here.

Golak: We'll be slaves, husband and wife. Our children?

Raavan: They'll be slaves too.

Golak: Their descendants?

Raavan: I'll buy them all up . . .

Golak: (singing) You're so kind, so kind, master
you've taken away from me the greatest care of all,

We'll never have to worry about our food again,
But, master, what's the price? . . .

Raavan: (in prose) . . . I'll give you three rupees. Have you ever seen three rupees in your life? D'you know the look of them?

Golak and his wife: (in thrilled disbelief) Three rupees! . . . It's too much. . . . Just too much. The master's going to buy us for three rupees. (39-40)

This passage is indeed a testimony to Mahasweta Devi's achievement as a dramatist.

In fact, Mahasweta Devi makes this passage reenact the simple but inexorably universal practice of enslavement of the famished and poor by the privileged in society for ages. The plain raw reality of this practice has made bondage a habit of the mind. The poignancy of the situation, although felt by the suffering humanity, has not made them desire freedom, for 'freedom' as a feeling or idea has never struck them. It is the supreme irony of this situation through history Mahasweta Devi seems to construct.

By letting the same character perform dual roles, Mahasweta Devi not only achieves theatrical economy but also tries to show a link between the past and the present. In fact, the device of a character in the present enacting a happening in the past, observes Samik Bandyopadhyay, is "a metaphor for the continuities in the process of exploitation." (xv)

Besides, the passage is significant for its novelty. It reminds us of a scene from any street play. In an interview to a Telugu daily, Mahasweta Devi admits that she is familiar with the street plays written and performed by Shibik Chandra whom she followed in Kerala where he made an effort to enlighten the downtrodden and the bonded labourers.[8]

As such, the transformation of a character takes place right in front of the audience. And a mere statement—"Please allow me to become my forefather"—is enough to suggest a change in time and place. Through Paatan's deliberate recall and enactment, the playwright seems to have emphasized "historicity over nostalgia." She concentrates more on the subject than on the theatrical properties. What matters is the direct communication of the subject between the audience and the actors. The same attitude can also be discernible in the dramatic work of Badal Sircar, one of the greatest contemporary dramatists. Sircar, like Mahasweta Devi, does not believe in the use of any kind of technique. He has developed his 'Third Theatre' which is inexpensive and does not have any external trappings like sets, lights, costumes, sound and make up which are necessary in a commercial theatre.[9] And his production can be performed anywhere. In his play *Michhil* (Procession), Sircar makes a dead character rise and speak directly to the audience: "I was murdered yesterday. Day before yesterday. And the day before that. . . . I am murdered everyday. Murdered everyday, dead everyday. I will be murdered tomorrow."[10] And it is this device which is also at work in Scene I, in *Aajir*. What both the characters in *Michhil* and *Aajir* are made to represent is a social reality that goes on everyday.

What makes Golak Kura, the ancestor of Paatan, doom his family to the life of aajirs is the fear of death. He enters into "an agreement for perpetual slavery . . . for the price of three rupees" (41) as he knows that

> There'll be drought every year
> There'll be famine every year, (42)

and that "brings death to all around."

Condemned to be a slave, Paatan is not entitled to any sort of enjoyment. All his human feelings are crushed ruthlessly. The paltry amount given in exchange for his life-long service symbolizes the inhuman status to which a person is reduced by poverty. A human being can be bargained away like an animal in a market. The society which is responsible for this situation, remains an indifferent spectator. Thus, the scathing remark made by Golak Kura at the end of the first scene is not unqualified when he says to the audience: "Did you hear that, you bunch of worms? . . . You can all go to your deaths. I'll have my three rupees." (40)

Interestingly, the amount of three rupees used again and again as a leitmotif in the works of literature seems to have acquired an added significance. In Mulk Raj Anand's novel *Coolie*, the protagonist Munoo is offered three rupees by his mistress: "Three rupees a month is a good wage, more money in fact than your mother or father ever saw."[11]

Both Anand's Munoo and Mahasweta Devi's Paatan are victims of poverty. While the former is in search of a job, the latter strives hard to get himself free from the conventional bondage. However, Paatan, unlike Munoo, does not yield to the circumstances.

In his struggle, Paatan is confronted with many a trying situation. He has borne the injustice meted out to him by the members of feudal world with a great fortitude. We are provided with an opportunity to have a glimpse of Paatan's physical strength not in terms of direction but in the words of his torturers. It seems, every alternate hour or day, Paatan gets a whipping at the hands of his master, Maatang Shunri: "What a body the bastard has! Strong as a horse! I beat him up, and it's my hands aching now." (42)

Although Paatan is endowed with such animal strength, he meekly submits to his master who is in no way a match to him. He is overwhelmed by a sense of fear—a fear of insecurity and of isolation. No wonder, within a system which denies the basic human rights, observes Aung San Suu Kyi, the Nobel Laureate, "fear tends to be the order of the day."[12]

The characters develop into full-fledged personalities as they involve themselves in the conversation that marks the progress of the play. We also, for the first time, learn of many hard facts about rural life that is India.

Through the system of contrasts and parallels, Mahasweta Devi tries to concretize in words the life she knows best. As such, Paatan becomes a happy contrast to his master, Maatang Shunri. Maatang is a typical member of the exploitative mechanism which is prevalent in the villages. He wields authority over the village-folk. Nothing is done without his participation. He is a cruel master and a professional womanizer. But, what is more surprising about him is that he is a henpecked husband. He is a butt of his wife's sarcastic comments. He fails to satisfy the sexual hunger of his wife (the Mistress) who secretly longs for the company of Paatan for she finds in him the potency which Maatang lacks. However, the Mistress does not let him know of her inner feelings, though she speaks in favour of Paatan whenever he is punished.

Maatang Shunri uses brutal force to suppress the tide of revolt surging forth in Paatan. He fears that Paatan may come to know of the secret of his bondage. He beats Paatan on the pretext that the latter dreams of freedom.

Maatang:	He's a horrible sinner.
The Mistress:	Why?
Maatang:	Why does he forget he's an aajir? His forefather sold him away. He wouldn't keep that in mind, he'd dream of marrying, having a family of his own, looking upon the face of his own son. (He spits on the ground.) Is there anyone who'd give away a daughter in marriage to an aajir? (43)

It reflects the height of inhumanity of the oppressor to which Paatan is exposed. Paatan is a creature to be pitied. He is not even allowed to fulfil his obligations. He wishes to marry only to please the souls of his dead ancestors. He says:

> I am an aajir, nobody'd marry me. My forefathers, denied the offering of water from their descendants, would burn in hell forever. (46)

Though it is this awareness of filial responsibility which initially makes Paatan think of marriage, it is a clear hint for revolt against the traditional constraints and a sure proof of realization of one's inalienable right to happiness. And from here, it does not require a very big step to watch Paatan, 'the common man hero,' evolving into an insurgent. Ranjit Guha maintains that "when a peasant rose in revolt at any time or place . . . he did so necessarily and explicitly in violation of a series of codes which defined his very existence as a member of that . . . semi-feudal society."[13]

The element of irony permeates the play. The Mistress of the house is sympathetic towards Paatan. She shows womanly concern whenever he is hurt savagely by her husband. And she makes him feel assured. It is this human touch in the Mistress which distinguishes her from Maatang, and makes her a lovable figure on the stage, although she aims at making Paatan alive to her lust. At times, moved by the pathetic condition of Paatan, she does not even hesitate to defy her husband. She is outspoken when she says:

> You're a clever fox! You tell Paatan you have his bond of slavery, and he doesn't dare run away . . . You tell me you've given my father a share of the cropland, you tell me you'll give me a son, you have a sop for everybody and then you go to Punnashashi's house and dance without a stitch on your back! (43-44)

Here, the Mistress seems to give vent to her inner agony. As a matter of fact, the Mistress, despite her opulent background, is not happy. She, like Paatan, is an object of pity. Also, she, like Sujata Chatterjee in *Mother of 1084* is a victim of male dominated society and patriarchal values.

The Mistress, married to Maatang, an 'old dotard' and a 'bloody eunuch,' feels an eternal sensual "fire burning within . . . a fire . . . that drives me diving into the slush again and again." (44) She asks: "Bangles on my wrist! Do they mean a thing when a young woman lusts for a man?" (44) So, the Mistress, realizing that Maatang could not quench her sexual thirst, and make a mother of her, she turns to Paatan:

The Mistress:	(tenderly) Paatan! Paatan! dear! (Paatan enters and stands, his head drooping.)
The Mistress:	Where did he hurt you, my child? (she strokes Paatan all over. She is . . . all flesh and craving. But Paatan remains unconcerned.)
Paatan:	I spoke of marrying, and he beat me up.
The Mistress:	Who 'd give you away in marriage, my child, unless it's me? Come, sit here by me. Come closer.
Paatan:	No, no. I look upon you as a mother.
The Mistress:	Then why don't you come closer to me?
Paatan:	You'll be a mother no longer, if I come too close to you.
The Mistress:	What do you feel then?
Paatan:	My body's aflame.
The Mistress:	What about mine? It's aflame all the time. (45)

For a slave like Paatan, it is a strange experience. He belongs to that section of society which, in its struggle to live by sheer "water drained from cooked rice," (41) has forgotten long ago to think of woman and sex.

However, ignited by the advances made by the Mistress, Paatan is in conflict with himself. He mutters to himself:

> I asked the Mother of the cremation ground: She is my lady the Mistress, I should look upon her . . . as a mother. Yet why does my body burn with passion whenever I come close to her? She told me: Son, if you are innocent nothing should affect you. . . . Son, if there's the touch of sin within you, and your body burns, bring devotion to your mind and quench the fire in its cool. (45-46)

The passage reflects the turmoil in the mind of Paatan. Perturbed though he is, he begins to yield to new demands within and without.

Interestingly, the Mistress, with all sensuality and seemingly immoral act of wooing Paatan, does not lose sympathy of the audience. She is one of the many tragic characters that Mahasweta Devi created in her writings. The words she is made to utter—"My body's loaded with diseases, Paatan, your master has made an aajir of you, and of me too (46)—are full of pathos. Besides, it is she who gives Paatan a new lease of life. She promises him that she will "steal your aajir's bond for you and give it back to you." (47) This situation in the play throws up the similarity and unity of the cause of aajir and of the woman.

Encouraged by the Mistress's promise, Paatan runs after a gipsy woman, who is a vendor of "all kinds of potions. Potions to bring to you whomever you desire." (47) He pleads with her to release him by marrying:

Paatan:	Take me away with you.
Gipsy woman:	Where can I go with an aajir? Wherever you go, they all drag you back and flog you to death.
Paatan:	The world's enormous! Purulia, Bankura, Dumka can be anywhere! . . . I'll make a home for us, we'll have son, I'll offer water to my forefather!

Gipsy woman: What'll you eat? Will you starve your life through?

Paatan: I bring all the money from my Master's brewery. (49)

But this adventure of Paatan is bound to fail. He has to pay for having dreamt of a new life. Surprisingly, the Mistress, who provokes Paatan, lets loose her men on him when she learns that she may miss him for ever. They drag him all along beating brutally. The description of the whole act of punishing Paatan is realistic: "Paatan falls, is beaten, rises to his feet, made to walk with voices off roaring 'stone him! stone him' Paatan seems to cower under a torrent of stones and writhes in pain as they hit him." (51)

Aajir is also remarkable for its poetry. The play is strewn with a number of songs and passages that bring out the poet in the playwright. Consider the episode of Punnashashi, in Scene 3. Punnashashi, a prostitute by profession, is again a victim of high-handedness of lusty agents of feudal institution. In order to propitiate the rain god, she is made to walk naked on a new moon night. She is poetic when she tells her tale of woe:

> I have to fast the day through and then roam through the night till the evening star crosses to the other end of the sky. . . . Isn't a whore's body a human body after all? You bastards, you had to tear me up, and then I have to fast without a drop of water. (Stops in her tracks.) O mother of cremation ground! Have mercy on me, and let me pray for water! (sings)
>
> Give us water, king Ind, give us water.
> The soil's parched in the dreadful drought.
> Let us have the frog couple married and let us sow the seeds.
> Give us water, king Ind, save our lives. (50-51)

The mob who caught Paatan, grow poetic as they enact the scene of punishing him:

> The world's not for you.
> The gipsy woman's not for you.
> As long as the aajir's bond's there.

> You're just a maimed beast,
> And Maatang's your God.
> The gipsy woman's not for you.
> The world's not for you.
> Life's not for you. (52)

By using songs, the playwright rather tries to make the audience react to the sufferings of the characters on the stage.

Paatan's hopes are dashed. In fact, he has few more surprises in store. He feels betrayed when he learns that the Mistress is a party to the conspiracy. He is further shocked to find the Mistress behaving unusually. The Mistress simulates high seriousness when she tells the mob:

> There's a funeral pyre burning within me, bastard! . . . (To the mob.) Tie him up with ropes and drag him along. I'll keep him tied to the post in my courtyard. Don't you know your ancestors have bound you as a slave from birth? I'll keep you tied in the courtyard and whipped with a new gaamcha [a piece of material like cheese cloth used mainly as a towel] I'd love to see your blood flow. I'll have my hands red with your blood and then go to sleep tonight. (53)

But, in reality, she wants to keep him to herself. She cannot stand Paatan leaving her for another woman. It is evident from the following conversation:

The Mistress:	I'll get you married. . . . Can you imagine what kind of a bride I'll choose for you?
Paatan:	(wrapped in a spell) What kind?
The Mistress:	A woman like me!
Paatan:	Like you!
The Mistress:	Yes a luscious woman. Luscious youth.
Paatan:	Like you!
The Mistress:	You wouldn't be satisfied with anything less! (46-47)

The Mistress continues wooing Paatan. She tries to convince him that she is for him. But Paatan remains unconcerned. He still regards her as a mother. However, it is difficult for one, observes Mulk Raj Anand, "to remain moral in an immoral world."[14] Mahasweta Devi seems to subscribe to this conception as she has Paatan respond positively. Having found the Mistress "all decked up in ornaments . . . inviting passionately, overpoweringly," Paatan says:

> All this jewellry. They're kept locked up in the Master's chest. Who are you? (Looks to the ground.) There's your shadow on the ground. So you must be the Mistress mother. (He lays his hands firmly on her shoulders, and roars at her.) When you come to me like this, you're no longer a mother to me, it's my blood that roars, and you drive me towards hell. (54)

Suddenly, Paatan comes to senses and feels that there's no 'escape' for him, because "where's there a place without a master, without the villagers, without you (the Mistress), without the aajir's bond? Where is there a country where the drought scorched people don't dance in glee at the sight of an aajir's blood?" (54-55) He is unable to relieve himself of the burden of the convention that has deprived him of all human joys. Having found no way to realize his dream of freedom, Paatan, in a fit of anger, cries out:

> (Rushes up to the front of the stage, and raises his eyes upwards.) Hey, you bastards, haunting the cremation ground! Why are you so thirsty? Weren't you born in the lap of famine, and didn't you die, in its lap? Then how can you be thirsty? (The wind wails) No. I won't marry ever. I won't continue a family of aajirs. You bastard, Golak Kura for a paltry three rupees you signed an aajir's bond and left generations enslaved for life. I'll bring your line to an end. If there's no death for the aajir's bond I'll finish it off with my death. (55)

It is the tone of a young man driven to desperation.

About this time, the Mistress's words of sympathy and her promise of setting him free raise Paatan's hopes again. In fact, all the apprehensions he has about the consequence of elopement with the Mistress have been subdued when the latter says that she brings with her the "aajir's bond bound in a gaamchha tied up to a band around" (55) her waist. Thus, motivated by a desire to live a human life in a world where class and status are obliterated and where everyone is regarded as human, Paatan ventures, by eloping with the Mistress, to defy not only the tradition but also the dictates of his conscience.

Ironically enough, the Mistress, who rouses the animal desire latent in Paatan to quench her insatiable hunger for sex, falls prey to her own wicked designs. In a sense, this unethical act of hers is both—yet another form of exploitation and revolt against patriarchal system.

When demanded to show the bond, the Mistress reveals the fact that there is no bond—"It is just a gaamchha (takes it out, shakes it), with the bond long turned to dust." (56) But Paatan does not believe it. He thinks that she has left it behind to have him flogged again. Suddenly, he is gripped by a fear—the fear of being thrown once again into the abyss of servitude. Justly, the playwright dramatizes his inner agony through a device of voices from an invisible chorus:

> An aajir, you! An aajir, you!
> No escape for you! No escape for you!
> No life for you! No world for you!
> An aajir, you! No escape for you! (57)

So, Paatan, in his anxiety to possess the bond before something worse befalls him, becomes aggressive. He holds the Mistress by throat and strangles her, shouting: "Give me the bond, you bitch! Tell me where you keep your key. Let me see for myself. Give me the key, the key!" (56)

The Mistress breathes her last. Although Paatan appears shocked at the unexpected turn of the situation, he becomes more assertive in his final confrontation with Maatang, who having found his wife dead, reveals that there has been no "aajir's bond": "I haven't seen it myself, my father hadn't seen it, it had turned to dust long ago in this gaamchha in which it had been once upon a time." (57)

The play comes to an end with Paatan realizing, "Like everyone else in the world, I was a free man (stating a fact), and I alone didn't know. (Looks at the dead woman. . . .) This luscious woman was for me, I didn't know." (58) This upholds the supreme irony of the situation with all its poignancy.

NOTES

1. Qtd. Samik Bandyopadhyay, "Introduction," *Five Plays*, by Mahasweta Devi (Calcutta: Seagull Books, 1986), p. xiii.
2. *Bonded Labour in India* (New Delhi: Uppal, 1982), p. 3.
3. Qtd. Spivak, "Notes for Anveshi/Subaltern Studies," p. 4.
4. Qtd. Bandyopadhyay, p. xiii.
5. G.J. Watson, "Shaw and Brecht," *Drama: An Introduction* (London: Macmillan Education, 1983), p. 163.
6. Harindranath Chattopadhyaya, *Five Plays* (Pondicherry, 1937), pp. 35-36.
7. Trans. Bandyopadhyay (Calcutta: Thema, 1990), p. 15.
8. "Kondakonala Velugu Dari Mahasweta Devi," *Udayam* (Telugu), Sept. 30, 1991.
9. Veena Noble Dass, *Modern Indian Drama in English Translation* (Hyderabad: Taurus, 1988), p. 67.
10. Badal Sircar, *Michhil*, trans, Samik Bandyopadhyay, in *Three Plays* (Calcutta: Seagull Books, 1983), pp. 6-7.
11. Qtd. C.D. Narasimhaiah, *The Swan and the Eagle* (Shimla: Indian Institute of Advanced Study, 1987), p. 119.
12. "Freedom from Fear," *The Hindu*, Feb. 28, 1993, p. ii.
13. "The Prose of Counter Insurgency," *Subaltern Studies* (Delhi: Oxford University Press, 1983), p. 1.
14. *Apology for Heroism* (New Delhi: Arnold-Heinemann, 1975), p. 20.

Urvashi O Johnny: The Rebel as Artist

Mahasweta Devi's *Urvashi O Johnny*, third play in the anthology, was a short story like *Aajir*, before it was rewritten as a play during the second phase of play-writing in 1976-77. In the earlier plays, Mahasweta Devi sought to throw light on the predicament of the individuals placed in different social situations. Even in the arrangement of her plays in the anthology, there appears an implicit design to ram home the varied forms of exploitation and oppression of the underprivileged. For, while *Mother of 1084* manifestly aims to reconstruct the events during the ruthless suppression of the Naxalite Movement and its impact on the lives of a cross-section of the survivors who bear the scars and wounds of those horrible days, and those who had lived through the days of violence in simulated insularity, the second play *Aajir*, set in the rural world, powerfully exposes the dehumanizing effects of the age-old conventions which have deprived the village life of its idyllic beauty and innocence.

And, interestingly, Mahasweta Devi again in *Urvashi O Johnny* moves back to the urban world exploring in depth the realities of the life lived on the streets of Calcutta which is one of the so-called developed state capitals in India.

Unlike in *Mother of 1084*, Mahasweta Devi, in *Urvashi O Johnny,* deals with "the roofless and the rootless" people whose pathetic existence has so far given other writers a scope for churning out fantastic stories only to amuse the well-fed and easy-going urban middle class readers. Thus, by writing this play, Mahasweta Devi seems to protest against the urbanites, who, engaged in the pursuit of the materialistic pleasure have become, insensitive and are reluctant to be stirred to life that is reality. It is, thus, also a satire on the pseudo-intelligentsia who, well aware of the causes of the sufferings of the underprivileged, sing to the tune of the establishment, instead of attempting to lead the masses to a new dawn of hope.

The play gives a lacerating account of the dehumanized existence of slum-dwellers in Calcutta. Although, as Samik Bandyopadhyay states, *Urvashi O Johnny* is Mahasweta Devi's play for the Emergency,[1] it acquires universality of appeal as it realistically portrays the unending and unmerited tortures to which the lowliest human being is subjected and which has been a common phenomenon in the whole of human history. Keeping in mind the horrors of the Emergency which "plunged the Indian sensibility" into "shock and pain and utter helplessness," (xiv) she focusses man's inhumanity to man. The vivid account of the sorrows and joys in the lives of what could be called the discards of society is characterized by the playwright's single-minded commitment and passion for the underdog which is an element rarely found in the works of the contemporary writers.

Interestingly, the thrust here, in fact, in the whole bulk of Mahasweta Devi's creative work, is the release of human soul from all kinds of oppression and exploitation. And she wants even the lowliest human being like beggar, who has virtually been denied a place among humans and considered to be a bruden of the society, to realize his/her self in the freedom the release affords. Self-realisation is man's highest value, and absolute value and it is this idea which is also central to her earlier plays—*Mother of 1084* and *Aajir*.

Brati Chatterjee of *Mother of 1084* wages a war against mighty exploitative mechanism. His mission in life is to emancipate the suffering humanity from the clutches of the oppressor. In his direct confrontation with the Establishment, Brati is killed. And, his mother, Sujata, fails to understand what he is really made of. She sets out in quest of her son's true-self, and she finds in his death an echo of her own silent protest against the patriarchal values.

The protagoinst, Paatan, in *Aajir* is a slave. Unlike his forefathers who served their masters faithfully, he craves for freedom. He leads himself to the altar of freedom by shattering all the constraints that incapacitate him for love and marriage.

With *Urvashi O Johnny*, Mahasweta Devi boldly attempts to confront an audience with its inhumanity towards a class of people whose tenuous relationship with the mainstream life has already begun to fade out. She creates a character in the play who, like Paatan of *Aajir*, is trapped in an excruciating situation from which he struggles hard to come out with an unfaltering faith in human dignity.

Johnny, the protagonist in the play, wishes to make every person happier with his tricks. In fact, he has been obsessed with a desire to take the suffering humanity to a paradise of freedom. Accordingly, he runs away, even when he is in his teens from all his mentors to "catch the birds of happiness and bring them to you." (80)

Away from his place, Johnny trains himself to be a ventriloquist and ventriloquism becomes his life-long obsession. Strangely enough, he becomes infatuated with the marionette which he considers to be a source of happiness for the audience and a means of livelihood for him. But in course of time he develops a cancer in the throat. Urvashi, the 'talking doll,' becomes mute because it is the voice of Johnny that she shares all along for the amusement of the audience that is people.

Johnny does not heed to the advice of doctor and his patrons who warn him that he would become dumb out and out if he continues to gab. We are provided with an opportunity for the first time, to watch how Johnny, the champion of the suffering brethren, is left with none, and how he transforms into a non-entity as he loses his voice which he uses to offer people, at least, a moment of release from the struggles of work-a-day world. However serious the consequences may be, Johnny does not give up his profession for he finds in it a form of freedom—a freedom of finding his joy and love in others. And the play ends with Johnny struggling to give his final show which, in fact, adds a new dimension to it.

Apparently, the structure of *Urvashi O Johnny*, like *Aajir*, is very simple. It is written in scenes. The dramatist does not use any overt technique. But her deft use of lighting makes the play effective on the stage. The effects, produced through lighting, at different times in the play help the audience to read the moods of the characters without the dramatist's intervention in the form of direction. Besides, gestures are also used throughout. Mahasweta links gestures with dialogue so that they make a more subtle impression. Mahasweta Devi's theatre, like that of Badal Sircar, is poor because it does not have external trappings like settings and other devices which are necessary in a commercial theatre. In her conception of such theatre, Mahasweta Devi appears to have been aware of Badal Sircar's familiar thesis: "We adopted the concept of poor theatre in the literal sense that is inexpensive theatre. Our group was poor, so are our countrymen, but we wanted to utilize poverty and turn into an advantage instead of a restriction."[2]

Urvashi O Johnny is essentailly a play of social realism. Social realism, observes K.A. Abbas, "is the acute awareness of the social forces that surround the individual, their power to influence the lives of men and women and overall interaction of individual and society."[3] Social realism, which gained initial momentum during the thirties, has been furthered by the 'convinced' left-oriented progressive intellectuals. In fact, social realism as a theatrical stylization is attractive to Mahasweta Devi because it has given her dramatic art verisimilitude, has infused her work with breath of life and has also allowed the maximum opportunity to comment.

With Johnny, Mahasweta Devi tries to focus the attention of the urban elite of Calcutta on the hidden realities which they are blissfully uaware of.

Johnny is an orphan. But, unlike many of those orphans who lead worse than a marginal existence in the slums and on the pavements of major cities, he strives to live the life of a respectable human being. His search for a happier life leads him to the profession of ventriloquism. Though at the outset, it serves as a means for him to earn a living, it becomes an obsession with him for he finds in it a suitable medium for self-expression. Johnny is seen on the verge of damnation when the play opens up:

Johnny: (addressing the audience, in English) Sirs and Madams . . . (in pidgin Hindi) Johnny pays his salaam to you. This is Johnny (He makes a low ceremonial bow, and dances a jig. Sings to the tune of the popular Hindi film song. . . . .

My shoes from the side walk,
my pantaloons from the sidewalk,
my vest and hankies stolen,
my cap I made myself!

(In prose) But who am I? (Goes close to Urvashi.)

Urvashi: (in a long drawl) My slave.

Johnny: (runs up down stage) Yes sir, I am her slave. Have been a slave for ages—her slave. Haven't you ever seen the play of Urvashi and Johnny? At the Gana Park, during the fair for Chadak, at the Hazra Park, on the sidewalk? Haven't you? I'm here to check in at the hospital and they wouldn't like me to gab too much. (61)

The passage which resembles the opening of *Aajir* exhibits all the remarkable features of Mahasweta Devi as a playwright. As an exposition, this passage unmistakably hints at the central conflict. In fact, by allowing the protagonist to directly address the audience, the playwright deliberately destroys theatrical illusion. However, here, the device of direct address to the audience does not aim to distract them from the stage, rather it forces them to respond immediately to the predicament of the character.

Sights like Johnny, with "a baggy, patched trousers, a coloured vest, a coloured handkerchief about his neck, a feathered cap on his head, and shoes" (16) are everyday presences in Calcutta. They are to be found everywhere like the garbage in the streets. One walks past them without feeling a twinge of guilt. They are part of Calcutta's landscapes.

Johnny, "son of the orphanage," is aware of the smothering effects of unethical social values. He runs away from all the forces that appear to curb his freedom and when he "was a young man . . . I took Urvashi on my lap and . . . in tongas to Jhansi, Laltapur, Banda, Hamirpur!" (71) He becomes, thus, a ventriloquist and since then he has been addicted to Urvashi. He tells the Doctor:

> You know quite well, Doctor, the show can't go on without Urvashi. She'll sing. She'll talk, she'll laugh. And the public'll ask. So, how are you, Urvashi? And she'll reply in great happiness. . . . I'm the Queen of Happiness. Johnny's kept

> me in great happiness. Take pity on me. . . . I'll strave if Urvashi doesn't sing or laugh anymore. (62-63)

And it is in this affair between 'animate and inanimate' that Mahasweta Devi "sees a desperateness, a life and death involvement that demands from the man a commitment more than human, and a commitment that eventually proves to be fatal." (xiv)

Like Brati Chatterjee of *Mother of 1084*, Johnny is a crusader for human rights. Preoccupied with a motive of altruism, he could not bear to see the weak and the hapless being subjected to innumerable indignities. He risks his personal enjoyments for the sake of the common good. We come to learn of Johnny's humanistic behaviour, when the One-Eyed Moti, a prostitute and his beloved, recounts how he rejected her love and made off to Bomaby to realize his dream of freedom:

> Aunt once asked Johnny to marry me. (She shakes her head sadly.) He wouldn't hear of it. Two of them ran away. (To Urvashi) They travelled through so many lands before they reached Bombay where they bought you off Hamid. And ever since he has been your slave. Eventually I became a whore, then I became old, and now I'm a slum owner. (72)

These lines help us to understand how the people, compelled by utter penury, take to dehumanizing work like prostitution.

A major part of Calcutta populace, which the urban elite insists on calling 'parasites,' have been confined to the pavements. They even appear to have been denied a right to live as equal citizens. Although the middle-class and the wealthy, and the economy more generally could not survive without them and their services, no genuine attempt is made to imporve their living conditions. On the contrary, remarks Jai Sen, they are not only "exploited but their lifestyles and livelihoods are often made illegal, and then even the 'illegality' is exploited."[4]

And the indifference of the urban rich to the suffering humanity is incarnated in the lifeless mass of buildings only matched by all the conventions or trappings of civilization that is social ethos, political awareness and spiritual apathy. This aspect is reinforced further by Calcutta being the capital city and representing the consciousness of the Bengalis which rode several movements, reforms, rebellions and revolutionary struggles. As the play progresses, it reveals to us many hard facts of life in the urban world. Johnny says to the One-Eyed one:

> Everyone seeks happiness. Even when they don't afford to go to the movies they watch the queue at the counter and draw happiness out of the sight. Before a sweetmeats shop, beggars . . . maimed in their arms and legs roll along the hot pitch begging for their masters and money-lenders, and find happiness in watching smart things. I showed the play of Johnny and Urvashi. (75)

At times, it is even to this sort of vicarious living that the people like Johnny have no access. Alienated from the mainstream life, they are forced to live a dog's life. Interestingly, we get a glimpse of true picture of the life of beggars in Calcutta, when Ramanna, the leper and the childhood companion of Johnny, reveals:

> No, tonight the lame one's gang will fight with Magandas' gang for their rights over the litter heap. We're in bad days, Johnny. When you see the beggars betraying their faith, that's a sign that the times have come to a monstrous state. The city belongs to the beggars. It's been all divided up. The lame one will pick up all the litter in the heap on the right and Magandas has the right to the heap on the left. But trust Magandas the bastard, he sneaks into the lame one's territory everday. He hasn't had a taste of the lame one's guts. Tonight the lame one will fight for the rights. (66)

It is not merely a comment on the condition of the helpless. It assumes metaphoric proportions, symbolizing soullessness of Calcutta and the degradation it unleashes.

The element of humour is a strong point of the play. Mahasweta Devi employs humour to provoke both thought and laughter. The conversation between Johnny and other characters, like Ramanna and the One-Eyed one, brings out the best in Mahasweta Devi as a playwright with a flair for humour. As Johnny says:

> It'll all be free service when Johnny's dead and Urvashi's dead. Everything for free. It's Laila-Majnu passing away, it's Heer Ranjha giving up the ghost, it's Shireen-Farhad popping off. Who'll ask for money? Once we are dead, there'll be no one left to raise laughters to sing. We'll carry away with us all the laughter, all the singing all the love-making of the city, all of that! (puts on his mask, and bows ceremoniously). (68)

And also consider this by Johnny: "What do the rich know of freedom? If the beggars had a four anna bit in their pockets, they could've put Calcutta up for auction any day." (75)

These passages not only make us laugh but also think. In fact *Urvashi O Johnny*, written during the Emergency, "an euphemism for state violence,"[5] undoubtedly reflects the trauma of the contemporary life which, stripped of its fundamental rights, has been given to despair. Man has been chained everywhere. He learns to live within the orbit of his private concerns. Thus, if Johnny says "Once we are dead there'll be no one left to raise laughter" and "what do the rich know of freedom?" he is merely stating the eternal facts. And his utterings such as "Money's never one's own. Money's a whore" (65) have a charming simplicity within the framework of dramatic action, giving elbow room for dramatic irony.

Johnny, in spite of being aware of his insecure social status, is committed to the cause of the suffering and struggling masses. He wants the people realize that "happiness is the greatest jewel one can find in life." (75) Unlike those disillusioned young men, who have confronted with established institutions which are bent on depriving the poor and needy of their due, Johnny aims at enlightening the masses by inculcating in them the spirit of freedom. In other words, it is rather a revolution of mind. He wants to make them aware of the nauseating conditions in which they are placed and which they are unmindful of. As Aung San Suu Kyi observes:

> The quintessential revolution is that of the spirit, born of an intellectual conviction of the need for change in those mental attitudes and values which shape the course of a nation's de-

> velopment. A revolution which aims merely at changing official policies and institutions with a view to an improvement in material conditions has little chance of genuine success. Without a revolution of the spirit of the forces which produced the inequities of the old order would continue to be operative, posing a constant threat to the process of reform and regeneration.[6]

To achieve this, Johnny chooses ventriloquism as his profession. In fact, ventriloquism is an acknowledged art form in our civilization and art has a role in realizing social as well as personal freedoms. But in the protagonist of this play, it cannot even earn him his daily bread. It is no more an enjoyable thing, instead it becomes a torture for him and a prop for beggary.

What really holds *Urvashi O Johnny* together as drama is Johnny's impassioned attachment to Urvashi, the marionette, which gains in metaphysical dimension as the latter begins to occupy his thoughts resulting in his total estrangement from his beloved, the One-Eyed Moti and his patrons who, having been conscious of the impending danger, persuade him to give it up. However much he might get infatuated with it, the marionette cannot be a substitute for his beloved. It is only a make-believe means for his happiness. It serves to highlight the fact that he is too poor to have a beloved and family. It is also an escape-route via art heightening the sense of unreality mixed with irony. Furthermore, the playwright endows Urvashi with the human qualities. It is around this inanimate character that the playwright revolves the entire drama of human relations by making its presence felt in almost all the scenes. In fact, all the characters including the protagonist address Urvashi in a language which we generally use when we speak to a fellow-being. And we are not informed that it is a marionette that Johnny is in love with till the end of the last scene which adds to the dramatic suspense of the play. The following conversation is typical of many:

Ramanna: Johnny?
Johnny: Yes?
Ramanna: I'm your true pal. Do you admit that?
Johnny: Of course. Certainly.

Ramanna: Give up Urvashi, pal.
Johnny: Why do you say that?
Ramanna: She'll finish you off.
Johnny: (breaks into a slow dance, singing to the tune of Mukesh a popular hit, Sansar hai ek nadiya; Life's a river. . . .)
I know it, Ramanna, I know it all,
Urvashi my beloved,
I've loved her all these days,
and the days have gone by in tears and laughter,
If I see her no more,
it'll be death for me, I'll drop dead, my man. (66-67)

Johnny's adoration of Urvashi, though appears to be abnormal and despite the ironies, is not without purpose. Johnny projects on Urvashi, the 'talking' doll, an image of romantic freedom by which he attempts to save both himself and the fellow beings from the danger of being overwhelmed by a sense of helplessness and grief, as he finds the true freedom nowhere near.

Symbolism also plays a part in the play. Urvashi, with a fixed smile on her face is a symbol of the 'dumb millions' who have been compelled to conform to the constricting ethics by putting on a cloak of happiness. And the efforts of Johnny, the representative victim of those ethics, to transform this frozen smile into a real laughter by lending his voice to Urvashi, become futile when he suffers from the cancer of throat, which, as Samik Bandyopadhyay rightly comments, is a metaphor for "the suppression of democratic rights." (xiv)

Mahasweta Devi's handling of the element of conflict in *Urvashi O Johnny* is effective. Johnny is torn internally by the conflict between the demand of self which craves for assertion and the demands of 'societal self' that the obligations be fulfilled. Johnny with a view to 'conquer happiness' leaves the One-Eyed Moti, who was "as beautiful as the moon once, the same as you all," (72) for Urvashi. However, he is not heartless. He feels that it is he who is responsible for her present condition:

Johnny: One-Eyed one? One-Eyed Moti?

The One-Eyed one:	Who's that? Is it Johnny? So you've come?
Johnny:	Why do you sing sad songs?
The One-Eyed one:	Because I don't know any songs of joy.
Johnny:	Go ahead, take me to task, lash at me, I can take all that, but I shake with fear when you talk of your sorrow. (73)

At the same time, Johnny knows what he is up to and he is determined to quest after the 'birds of happiness' "fluttering in the woods . . . reeling in the woods" (74) to get rid of the sorrows of the masses. When the One-Eyed one asks him if he had ever tried to respond to her love, he confesses:

> You stayed your life in Calcutta, you never knew what happiness means, one-eyed one. . . . I did. I would address them, you, citizens of the sidewalk, you need happiness most. I'm Johnny. I'm here to seek out for you from all over the world the birds of happiness. (73)

What is more surprising about *Urvashi O Johnny* is its world of characters. Unlike Asif Currimbhoy's *The Hungry Ones*, which deals with only an aspect of life of beggars in riot-torn and famine-stricken Bengal, Mahasweta Devi's *Urvashi O Johnny* is a play solely about beggars and their joys and sorrows.

Undoubtedly, the play gives us an insight into the life in Calcutta, which resembles the "Yaksha Town" in *The Red Oleanders* by Rabindranath Tagore where "The shadow Demon, who lives in the gold caves, has eaten into it. It is not whole itself nor does it allow anyone else remain whole."[7] It is indeed true that the mainstream life, eaten into its vitals by the devil of selfishness, has become soulless and faceless. And it is the callousness of the city, which is reflexive of its civilization, is insurmountable for an oppressed being like Johnny that he cannot see for himself an opportunity of realizing his own being.

On the contrary, the relations among the people who are generally denied the status of human being, have been humane. Each character in the play, however minor it be, comes to life with it being alive to the human passions such as love, hatred and anger.

which have been long forgotten by its counterpart in the so-called elite society. Thus, within the simple structure of the play, we notice a number of little contrasts and parallels which indicate that behind the apparent simplicity of structure there is a clarity of vision. And what makes a mature artist of Mahasweta Devi is her use of a situation to evoke another which is diametrically opposite to it.

Scene 4, which opens on One-Eyed Moti who "sits downstage dozing and singing . . . with Urvashi half reclining, indistinctly seen against the wings in the darkness," (72) presents a poignant picture of poverty-stricken slum life in Calcutta. The One-Eyed Moti still longs for Johnny, even though she knows of his commitment. Her heart is filled with love for him. She is moved to pity, when Johnny suffers the torments of putrefying body. In her long soliloquy, she gives vent to her inner agony. She squarely blames Urvashi:

> Why doesn't Johnny come? (Addressing Urvashi) you witch! You won't look after him. you won't leave him to me. If you gave him to me, I'd treasure him. (Swats a mosquito on her leg.) And these mosquitoes! You can't escape them, with twelve families clustering in the slum, with a single washroom! They let their children shit right at the doorsteps. A real hell, what hell! (Addressing Urvashi) Why don't you die, you witch? Johnny and Ramanna, do you know, were on the payroll of my aunt? (72)

This is the tone of a woman who has lost all her youth in waiting. She fails to realise her cherished dreams. She becomes a victim of perverted morals of modern society. A little later, we find the One-Eyed one and Johnny reminiscing:

Johnny:	Your aunt asked me to marry you.
The One-Eyed one:	You didn't. I remember everything. (With a sigh) You, Ramanna, and I went to see the film Ratan. Then we sat under the monument. Ramanna and you cut your hands with a dagger. let your bloods mingle to swear the oath

	that whoever survived would give the other one his last rites. Then you told me such a lot of things.
Johnny:	Tell me.
The One-Eyed one:	I wept. You dried my eyes. You told me. Don't one-eyed one. I'm not leaving you because you are one-eyed. I'm going off to bring back happiness. (74)

Fated as she is to put up with uncongenial and inhuman circumstances, the springs of human love in the One-Eyed one are unpolluted. She is still capable of her moments of compassion and charity. It is this human touch which makes most of Mahasweta Devi's characters likeable. When Johnny makes some incriminating comments about her profession, she instead of losing her temper, feels pity for his predicament.

Johnny:	When you die, it'll be only the scavenger who'll come to collect you. The government will requisition the slum. A whore's estate goes to the government.
The One-Eyed one:	(hurt deeply) What—at? How could you be so vicious? You're a lost one yourself. She's finished you off. (Points at Urvashi) Devil! Devil! Devil! (Pause. Then in a soft voice) There's some syrup for you. Take it before you go to sleep. You have your show tomorrow. (75)

Motivated, thus, by a sense of sympathy for the suffering humanity, Johnny sacrifices himself. He becomes a slave to Urvashi. He loves his profession of ventriloquism more than anything else. In the course of time, a disease, "never heard a thing like that," (64) which will "all turn to a corpse just a corpse" (71) attacks Johnny's throat "through which she [Urvashi] sings and speaks." (71)

By endowing *Urvashi O Johnny* with passages of poetic beauty and a number of popular songs, Mahasweta Devi has achieved the depth and intensity which otherwise would have been impossible.

Very often, the characters in the play burst into songs, which contain suggestive and trenchant comments on their action and character. But as Samik Bandyopadhyay rightly points out: "the magic of the popular songs with their sentimentality, and the painful naivete that can only mean death." (xiv)

However, it is only natural that the people, who have been swayed by nothing but a sense of sympathy and a zest for life, are stirred to action, whenever they find a fellow being suffer for no fault of his. And thus, the human passion, gushing forth, as it were, from their hearts, is transferred to song.

Moved by Johnny's helpless condition, Ramanna, a minor character in the play, sings to the tune of "Chalte Chalte Mere Yah Geet Yad Rakhna/ Kabhi Alvida na Kahna":

> Cancer in the throat,
> Never heard a thing like that,
> Don't give me cancer, my man,
> Don't give me cancer, my man, . . .
> If it's cancer,
> It gives the stink of the rotting corpse,
> It's the stink that tells,
> Don't give me cancer, my man. (64-65)

In Scene 3, we find Johnny, Ramanna and the lame one, a beggar-lord, together dancing and singing to the tune of another popular song from *Laila Majnu*:

> O Ruler of the skies, why does your world put me in a fix?
> Why does all the moonlight of the world turn to clouds for Johnny?
> Hey master, why expose Johnny to the masquerade?
> O Ruler of the skies, why does your world put me in a fix? (69)

When the words fail to convey their inarticulate feelings, the characters act them out. For instance, when the lame one suspects that someone must have struck Johnny with "the unseen arrow" causing him a dreadful cancer of the throat, Johnny and Ramanna do not speak but make gestures in agony as is evident from the direction:

> They touch their chests, and mime being hit by arrows, flutter their arms like wings, run around the stage in an act of agony, and come back to take their position downstage. (69)

Through this device—the device of giving a character action rather than speech—Mahasweta Devi makes the action still more eloquent.

Like in *Aajir*, in *Urvashi O Johnny*, Mahasweta Devi seeks to create a realistic atmosphere on the stage by being faithful to the lifestyles of the characters she deals with. And, at no place do we notice any character using a language other than the one which is akin to his or her occupation. In fact, the playwright uses the dialogue simply and effectively, allowing it to be shaped by the characters' essential personality. The uncouth expressions like 'bastard' and 'motherfucker' are used commonly. An example can be seen in the following dialogue:

Ramanna: Urvashi's a witch, the Devil's accomplice, a djinn. In Bombay, you stuck a knife into Hamid's heart, and ran away with her. Hamid wept and wept, till he drank himself to death. Urvashi will kill you too.

Johnny: (grimly) I'll finish her off before that . . . I'll drive the dagger first into Urvashi's breast, then into mine. Will you come with me?

Ramanna: I'll come with you. But you're a bastard. How can you put a dagger through Urvashi's breasts like apples that sell at ten rupees for a kilo? (67)

Using crude and abrasive language, Mahasweta Devi, unlike other dramatists, does not intend to shock the audience. In an article "Untapped Resources," Mahasweta Devi maintains:

> Using dialect, or the specific idiom of their language, the way they form sentences, is necessary because it enriches language. . . . But the slang and four-letter words are used frequently by common people not to shock, but to express emotion. . . . The living language of the common people,

> tribal or not, is a must for my kind of literature. This richness of language has not been exploited enough.[8]

At the end of Scene 4, Johnny, for a moment, feels sad that the people whom he wished to save, have turned him down, and he thinks that he has none except Urvashi to turn to. When he is all alone on the stage, he professes his love for Urvashi and continues to dote on her:

> (addressing the mask): Why are they all hitting out at me today? The lame one said, someone must've struck me with the unseen arrow. The one-eyed one says, you're a lost one, Johnny. (Goes upto Urvashi) Urvashi, my darling, I'm here. Your slave waits for your orders. (Salutes her.) What's the matter darling? Are you angry? (Pause) The lame one doesn t know anything. She says it's the unseen arrow. What non-sense? All that bash! . . . You know you're the only one I have in this wide world. (Moves closer to Urvashi, kneels before her.) How can you be so heartless? You won't speak to me at all? (75-76)

Disappointed and dejected, Johnny takes to boozing which gives him a momentary relief from his troubling conscience. But, all the same, he suffers from hallucinations. He hears mocking sounds from invisible persons. His inner conflict is externalized. This is achieved through a device of mask. Surprisingly enough, a fine spectacle of human drama is evoked by confronting the protagonist with a mere "row of masks . . . showing their teeth" (76) representing individuals from whose bondage he escaped and who he deceived from time to time only to "conquer happiness." The protagonist's rationalization for his action comes in a series of rhetorical questions addressed equally to himself and to the audience:

> (trying to convince the unseen contenders. . . . Runs around the stage. The derisive laughter continues and the heckling: "Get lost, you lost! out of the game!") Who's there to defeat me! Tell me! Yes, this is Johnny. Degenerates! Didn't I catch the birds of happiness and bring them to you? Who am I?

> Urvashi's my mistress, I'm her slave. Don't you know us? (The masks shake their heads in denial, they say: No.) (77)

In spite of being warned, Johnny renews his commitment to Urvashi. He sticks to the guns to the end. He feels that the whole world has conspired to separate Urvashi from him. The more he is threatened, the fiercer he becomes in his commitment to the cause of humanity. Thus, he prepares himself for the "last show of the season" (78) which, symbolically turns out to be the last performance of his life. The play comes to an end with Johnny's moving revelation through Urvashi—"only a marionette." (80)

> I'm not well, my dear public. I've cancer in my throat, my voice goes mute. There's cancer there—I'll never laugh again, never sing again, never talk again—the Urvashi who'd catch the birds of happiness and bring them to you is not in happiness any more. . . . How can you remain any longer? (After a pause one word at a time.) My voice. Has. Been. Taken. Away. For. Ever. All. Yours. Happiness. (80)

Thus, Johnny's pains and predicaments are not merely individualistic, his marionette being an artistic escape route or a surrogate of poverty. His cancer is not merely his, it is also the cancer of every one of the exploitative world itself.

But, despite these ironies which tend to mystify the protagonist in *Urvashi O Johnny* is to be looked at as ventriloquist with a purpose. He wished to use his art to awaken the oppressed to freedom from bondage, and oppression, and to lead them to a final confrontation with the oppressor. He becomes a victim of a terrible cancer of the throat. Though the voice he lends to the marionette to lure the "birds of happiness" to the den of suffering humanity has gone mute for ever, the dream of Johnny to make the audience more articulate in their expression of protest against oppression appears to take shape when the latter becomes more inquisitive for the first time: "What's the matter? Why did you fall silent? . . . Why is Johnny crying? Urvashi, how are you? How are we? Speak aloud, the way you always do. . . . What's wrong? . . . What's the matter? What's happened?" (79-80)

NOTES

1. Samik Bandyopadhyay, introduction, *Five Plays* (Calcutta: Seagull Books, 1986), p. xiv.
2. Badal Sircar, *The Third Theatre* (Calcutta, 1978), p. 26.
3. K.A. Abbas, "Social Realism and Change," *Aspects of Indian Literature: The Changing Pattern*, ed. Suresh Kohli (Delhi: Vikas, 1975), p. 146.
4. Jai Sen, "Unintended City," *Economic and Political Weekly*, Vol. XII, No. 15 (1977), p. 594.
5. Arun Sinha, "Violence against the Poor," *Economic and Political Weekly*, Vol. XII, No. 15 (1977), p. 594.
6. "Freedom from Fear," *The Hindu*, 28 Feb. 1993, p. 11.
7. Rabindranath Tagore, introduction, *The Red Oleanders* (Madras: Macmillan India, 1973).
8. Mahasweta Devi, "Untapped Resources," *Seminar*, 359 (1989), p. 19.

Bayen:
A Portrait of the Rebel as Mother

Before it was dramatized during 1976-77, Mahasweta Devi's *Bayen*, the fourth play in the anthology, had appeared, like most of her plays, as a short story in 1971. Here in the play, like in *Aajir*, Mahasweta Devi deliberately turning to the rural world, attempts to bring to light the realities "outside the pale of respectable existence."1 She also attempts to show in the play how the monstrous exploitative mechanism, stretching its ugly tentacles all over, reduces the human being to the level of mere beast. In the previous play, *Aajir*, which has the rural Bengal as its setting, the playwright reveals to us how the rural folk, struck by terrible poverty, has entered into perennial servitude since time immemorial.

Like *Mother of 1084, Bayen* is concerned with a mother who is caught in a trap laid by the vested interests. It is a fine study of the effects of the exploitation—political, social and economic—on the psyche of a sensitive individual who is essentially humane.[2]

Interestingly, the major portion of Mahasweta Devi's creative writings has been devoted, particularly, to expose the inhuman subjugation of women; and their struggles for survival, although they do not conform to any school of feminism. As compared to men, women become "the softest targets for the great upholders of the traditional values"[3] and are subjected to all kinds of humiliations. Being relegated to the position of mere "merchandize and commodities,"[4] the women are compelled to lose their identity. And, interestingly, it is in search of the identity that Mahasweta's characters set out and become martyrs.

But, in fact, Mahasweta Devi's protagonists, unlike those portrayed in the contemporary works of other writers who have been preoccupied with existential problems of the modern world, are not afraid of the harsh realities of life. They do not yield to the forces of the society in which they live. Rather, they struggle hard to make their mark by exhibiting exemplary courage and moral strength even in the face of hostile climate of stifling conventions. Samik Bandyopadhyay comments: "Two classes of characters that have dominated Mahasweta Devi's stories and novels in the seventies are the mothers bearing the brunt of social and political oppression, and enduring and resisting with indomitable will." (ix) He states further that they "are too earthy and emotionally charged to bear overtones of any mystical-mythical or archetypal motherhood. They are invariably located within a network of relationships defining their personalities into absolute clarity." (x)

Sujata Chatterjee, the protagonist in *Mother of 1084* is a victim of patriarchal authority of her husband. Despite her affluent background, she takes up a job in the bank as an act of self-assertion against oppression. However, she suffers patiently all the humiliations by her overbearing husband and corrupt children and their spouses till one morning when she is summoned to identify her favourite son Brati's dead body in the police morgue. In a series of encounters with the people who know Brati's mission and for whose sake he died, she discovers for herself the enormous spread of the power that she had so long identified with her dehumanized household alone. And she fnds in his sacrifice an articulation of her silent resentment she bears all along against the insensitive establishment and revolts.

Mahasweta Devi's *Bayen* really deals with a mother who is branded as a witch and separated from her family and society.

The practice of witchcraft, based mainly on the ignorance of the people and the vested interests, has been in vogue all over the world from ancient times. Particularly, the women of the oppressed sections, who are alleged to have been possessed by evil spirits, practise necromancy, that is, raising of the dead. Necromancy had justification in the medieval times as the act of Satan. And the existence of Satan as anti-God was essential for religion and Church and so necromancy and witchcraft came to be looked upon as necessary complements for faith.

And the religion in its positive aspect of worship of God and its negative dimension of the espousal of devil was also an instrument of exploitation. Therefore, it was enjoined on the subject class that is the oppressed as a duty towards God, Church or Temple and the king. Its negative complement was an additional means of damning the spirit of women of the working classes who had plenty of pluck and creative energy lent them by labour and kept them free from constricting prejudices, superstitions and dogmatism. To sum up, witchcraft was made use of as a vicious instrument to take away the freedom of the working class.

Even in twentieth century, many ignorant people believe in the reality of witchcraft. And 'witchcraft presecution,' which began in Europe about the close of the Middle Ages, has been still prevalent among uncivilized peoples of the world. Especially in the Santhal areas of Bengal in India, witch-hunting or witch-branding, a social evil, ever growing, like a cancerous ulcer on the face of rural life, is an excuse discovered by the vested interests to kill the innocent people and grab their property. Mahasweta Devi is reported to have confessed:

> Any strange thing or event can be attributed to the 'witches' and they can be killed with popular 'approval.' . . . Majority of the victims are women and it is estimated that 600 women are killed annually on this charge.[5]

In *Bayen*, probably, set against this background of the barbaric practice, Mahasweta Devi evolves an intensely human story, touching on the larger space of the social forces that separate mother and son in a male-dominated society.

The protagonist, Chandidasi Gangadasi, in *Bayen* is a professional gravedigger. Her work is to bury the dead children and guard the graves at night. Married to Malindar Gangaputta, an employee in the morgue, she becomes a cynosure of the village. Besides, "there was no one as beautiful as she, no one with such grace." (86) She is a tender-hearted mother. She takes utmost care of the dead children she buries. But, as time passes, she is fed up with her job. Having found in the corpses of infants an image of her own suckling child whom she has to leave for the graveyard at night, she feels disturbed. She wants to leave the profession which she has inherited from her great grandparents—the lords of the graveyard!

The privileged who, belittled by the prominence of her household, wait for an opportunity to strike—the way they always strike. They start thinking that she is responsible for the death of children. At times, they even throw stones at her. So she pleads with her husband to take her away from the village. But her grievances are unheard. Motivated by a sense of duty, she accepts to perform the last rites of a dead child of her relatives, who initially blame her for their misfortune. Thus, Chandi, while discharging her duties, is caught unawares and branded as a witch by the agents of feudal system. She is mercilessly separated from her son and family and is denied entry into the village. She has to live all by herself away from the feudal society, for her presence is considered ominous.

However, Bhagirath the son, though warned, visits her and learns about the reality of his mother. With his arrival, Chandi's relations with humanity are reestablished. And she dies averting a train accident which otherwise would have resulted in great death toll. The play comes to an end with Bhagirath acknowledging the dead as his mother which, being an act of revolt against the dead conventions, gives the play a new dimension typical of Mahasweta Devi's dramatic vision.

Structurally, *Bayen* is astonishingly simple. The play, consisting of 20 pages in all, is divided into four short well-wrought Brechtian scenes, with a beginning, middle and an end. Malindar Gangaputta's confrontation with Bayen and his revelation to Bhagirath constitutes the beginning of the play. Enactment of the whole process of dreadful expulsion of Chandi from the village forms the middle of the play. And Chandi's sacrifice and Bhagirath's defiance of the established morals of the society form the end of the play.

Mahasweta Devi, like in the preceding plays, has not employed any sort of technique, though a device of 'recalling' is put to use in the latter part of Scene 1 and in Scenes 2 and 3. The play moves with ease from the present to the past and back to the present, as the central character, Malindar, deliberately recalls and enacts very much like Paatan in *Aajir*. The device of a character in the present performing an incident in the past, by changing roles right in front of the audience, not only allows the playwright to present different dramatic situations without any recourse to superfluous scenic displays but also assures the smooth flow of action, touching the play with an element of authenticity.

Besides, the play, as in folk theatre, uses very few stage properties. The bare stage allows the playwright to telescope time and space. Freed of the burden of conventional theatrical trappings, the actors easily manipulate the same space to represent different locales. And a shift in scene is indicated by dropping the curtain.

Endowed with an authentic rural atmosphere, *Bayen* depicts the effects of superstitions on the innocent people. Notwithstanding the so-called scientific enlightenment, there is still a large part of Indian life which is sunk in ignorance and superstition. Besides, the agents of the corrupt feudal system, which is still in full control of the rural life, exacerbate the situation further.

The most dominating character in the play is Chandidasi Gangadasi. The world she belongs to is a far cry from that of Sujata Chatterjee in *Mother of 1084*. Unlike Sujata, she comes of a family of Domes who have been hailed as 'harijans' (Gandhi's 'respectable' term for the low caste untouchable). In fact, with Chandi, the dramatist seeks to reveal to us the *other* India where the people, ignorant of the radical changes brought about by different movements in the mainstream society, still experience the trauma of oppression reminiscent of the colonial rule. The personal freedoms of the individuals are ruthlessly crushed to the pleasure of the oppressor who assumes different roles—moneylender, zamindar and Jotedar.

The protagonist, Chandi, like Sujata, is a loving mother and a sensitive wife. She is a gravedigger by profession. She is entrusted to bury the dead children and guard the graves during night, as she is the progeny of the illustrious Kalu Dome who has been assigned to look after "all the cremation grounds of the world." (88) When King Harishchandra lost his kingdom and fell on evil days, it was Kalu Dome who provided him with food and shelter. Ironically, when he became king again, he had gifts for all and sundry "who never cared for you when you were in misery." (87) Malindar recalls how Kalu Dome, for his magnanimity towards the king, was rewarded:

> (He comes to the centre of the stage, turns his back to the audience, raises his face and shouts.) What have you for us? For my community?—A rich sombre voice makes a formal announcement.
> All the cremation grounds of the world are yours . . . yours, yours, yours, . . . Then Kalu Dome danced like this. (He raises his arms, and dances, screaming continuously.) The Brahmans, the sadhus, the sanyasis get cattle, land and gold, and we get all the cremation grounds of the world. (87-88)

It is evident that the process of subordination and exploitation of the underdog started long ago and the myths and legends, created by the bourgeois intellectuals are intended only to support the doctrine that one class is superior to the other.

Obliged to continue the conventional profession, which, in fact, does not befit a woman with a tender heart, Chandi is caught in a situation like that of Paatan in *Aajir*. However, unlike Paatan, Chandi is not a slave out and out. She carries out her obligations as a sign of reverence for her forefathers. There is a sense of purpose in her acceptance of the job. In other words, she has knowingly sacrificed what Freud called the 'pleasure principle' for the sake of the larger good of the community of which she is a part. Moreover, there are other reasons to go on with her job as she tells her husband:

> Whenever I seem to have made up my mind that I won't go back to the job ever, I seem to hear my father's voice roaring like thunder: If you opt out, it'll be my beat again, is that what you desire? Would you like me back on the job guarding the graves from the predatory jackals? I can almost hear him chasing the jackals away, thundering all the while, hoi! hoi! hoia! (92)

Chandi, an intellectually inferior woman, unlike Sujata, never tries to suppress her inner desire for freedom. She resents whatever she thinks might do harm to her sentiments. The seeds of conflict within herself between a committed mother and professional gravedigger as well as the larger confrontation between the womanhood and the forces of male-dominated society are sown.

So long as she remains unmarried, there is no real anguish in Chandi. She never experiences any inner conflict. As a responsible human being, she shows boundless enthusiasm for her work. She feels proud of being a gravedigger and is conscious of her social status among her own tribe. She tells Malindar when he proposes to her: "I'm Chandidasi Gangadasi. My father, the late Patitpaban Gangadhar. I bury dead children and guard the graves. . . . Kalu Dome's my forefather. I'm at the top of the Domes here." (89)

The playwright has endowed Chandi's character with the essential human qualities—an intense love for life and a sense of sympathy for the suffering humanity. We are provided with an insight into the beauty of the innocent life, lived in the lap of nature when Malindar enacts the love affair between him and Chandi in order to reveal the true identity of the latter to his son, Bhagirath:

Malindar: It was then, on the holiday, that I saw her first. (Pause. Pleadingly) Why don't you slip out for a while, child? Your father and mother will meet now, fall in love, get married and then you'll be born. (Shoves him out.) You shouldn't be watching this. (Bhagirath leaves the stage) Let me walk back to twelve years ago. (Walks. As he walks, he uses his fingers to rearrange his hair, rearranges his dhoti to a more youthful tightness.) Let me dance. . . . Chandidasi, also drunk, enters dancing.

Chandi: (Singing) It's black I love.
Krishna's black, the tamal tree's black, that's why it's black I love. It's black I. . . . (noticing Malindar) who are you, dear? My dark, dark lover? Haven't you had your booze? Aren't you drunk enough?

Malindar: (Singing) My Radha's fair, the lotus is fair. It's the fair I love.

Chandi: Great, darling, great! (Sings) Krishna says, it's time for holy, But where do I get my colours?

Malindar: (Sings) I'll steal the colours off your heart, dear, and pour it all over you.

Chandi: (Sings) I won't let you, I won't.

Malindar: (Sings) I won't let you go, I won't. (88-89)

Mahasweta Devi, as mentioned earlier, has been aware of the influence on the general public exerted by the street theatre in vogue. Apparently, the passage, modelled on a scene from a street play, is a good example of the craftsmanship of Mahasweta Devi as playwright. By letting the character transform, in full view of the audience, to enact an episode in the past, she, like Brecht, intentionally creates an antidote to the theatrical illusion which makes the audience respond intellectually to the action of the play and question it, instead of responding emotionally and accepting it. As the barriers between the audience and what happens on the stage are reduced to naught, the former is always aware that it is sitting in a theratre.

Chandi is envied for more reasons than one. Her husband, Malindar, is the only person who knows how to sing among the Gangaputta tribe. He has got a permanent job in the morgue and "built a new hut, and had two bighas of land for share cropping, how could they help being envious?" (91) However, she is not happy. She feels hurt that people suspect her of having an evil eye. She tries to break free from the obligations of her profession thrust on her by the feudal society. In fact, she has other reasons for her aversion to the job. She is now a mother of a handsome child. She tells:

> It hurts to do the job these days, the job handed down to me by my ancestors, my hands rebel. . . . Why can't you see it, Gangaputta, why I think throwing up the job again and again? when I guard the graves through the night, my breasts bursting with milk for my Bhagirath back home, all by myself. I can't, can't stay from him. (91-92)

It is this motherly concern for her child that inspires Chandi to go on with her job and lands her in a situation which leads to her estrangement from the feudal society and eventual rebellion.

The element of irony works effectively in *Bayen*. Mahasweta Devi brings together contradictions and disagreements. Chandi feels disgusted with her profession of burying dead children. Yet she cannot give it up. She pleads time and again with her husband to take her away to a place where she can lead a happier life looking after her little son. At the same time, she realizes her responsibilities as a gravedigger when she learns that a child of her relatives is dead.

Insensitive though he is, Malindar Gangaputta is aware of Chandi's charming personality. He prides himself on having married "a golden doll of a wife, a descendant of the great Kalu Dome." (91) He is a man of straw and embodies all the characteristics of the typical modern man who, engaged in the rat race of the mundane world, has forsaken human values and leads a compromising life. Malindar has taken a fancy to the glitter of the material world. He wants to live a class above his own by working hard. Despite all his enthusiasm and love for his wife, he turns out to be a little more than a conventional husband. Though he raves, at times, against those who speak ill of Chandi, he does not care for what is really eating her. Having failed to make out Chandi's request for her release from the conventionalities of life, he rather encourages her to carry on with her work.

Malindar: That's one thing you have, to harp on . . .
Chandidasi: . . . Listen to me, if I don't do it. . . . Oh why did God have to throw me into such quandary?
Malindar: Quandary? What's the quandary? When a child dies, can anyone keep it in the house? The job you do is a useful one, but the bastards won't recognize that. (91-92)

The unique feature of Mahasweta Devi's dramatic world is its women characters. She has a way of making her characters so alive; they tug at the heart. Her women are undoubtedly stronger characterizations as compared to men, who are often portrayed as lacking in insight into what is happening to their being. They remain, as it were, passive spectators as their counterparts pass through the painful situations created by an equally indifferent establishment. As a matter of fact, they are conformists to the hilt.

In Scene 1, we are provided with an opportunity to see how Malindar, though temporarily, feels guilty of treating Chandi brutally:

> (Covers his face with his hands, and cries bitterly) How could I do it? I hurled stones at her body? It used to be a body soft as butter. How could I be such a beast? . . . I'll go to the market, buy her things that she needs, and I leave them at her house. She has been starving since Thursday. It's Saturday today. (86)

It is this awareness of his guilt which makes Malindar more pathetic figure than Chandi on the stage. Surprisingly, though deep down in his heart he feels sympathy for her plight, he is miserably helpless. He never ventures to protest the tradition which is all set to wreak havoc on his family. His thoughts and feelings are regimented. He learns to make compromises at every stage and adds indirectly to the woes of Chandi. When asked why Chandi has to become a Bayen, he tells Bhagirath, without any hesitation: "Our bad luck, hers, yours and mine." (87)

On the contrary, Chandi is a woman of complete integrity. She is a lover of freedom, unfettered by the social constraints. She cannot brook to watch anyone suffer and goes out of her way to help them out. In fact, with the strong moral fibre of a true rebel, she violently resents any kind of encroachment on her freedom. Interestingly, what makes for tragedy in her life is her being a wife of an insensitive husband. Actually, Mahasweta Devi's mothers are always as much the victims of indifference of their household as of the society in which they live.

Evidently, Scene 2 deals with the central conflict of the play. Chandi appears to be at odds with herself. She is torn by the conflict between the societal self and the personal self. As a socially responsible person, she realizes the significance of her work. But as a wife and a mother, she has a greater role to play. There is also a conflict between Chandi and Malindar on the one hand and between her family and the social forces represented by Gourdas, the archetypal exploiter, on the other. Witness the opening conversation of Chandi with her child:

> Bhagirath, your father hasn't two minutes to spare to listen to my woes. Won't you listen to all that hurts within me? (She strokes the sleeping child.) Before you were born. I

> never knew I'd feel like this. Now it hurts so bad when I bury the little ones under the banyan tree. O my son, do you feel your mother's woe? Men in general are so insensitive. Their children die. I bury them. And they say I have the evil eye; if I stare at a child, it's sure to die. (Smiles sadly.) The other day in the dark someone hurled a stone at me! (90)

It is the voice of a frustrated woman. Here, indeed Chandi speaks for the dramatist herself. By putting the words "Men in general are so insensitive" into the protagonist's mouth, Mahasweta Devi seems to lash out at the men whose passivity, and inarticulateness have caused irreparable damage to the spirit of womanhood. Thus, the words, spoken out of boredom, actually reflect the predicament of Chandi, that is, of every mother. Symbolically, the child with its primal innocence serves as a link between the active world of Chandi and inactive world of Malindar. Here we are also, by implication, for the first time, informed that Chandi's confrontation with the superstitious people—'Someone hurled a stone at me'—is imminent.

As a character, Chandi has an edge over other characters. Unlike Sujata in *Mother of 1084* and Paatan in *Aajir*, she does not mince words and is more eloquent and fearless in her expression of protest against injustice. When people begin to suspect her motives, she has no other person than her husband to turn to for moral support. No doubt, Malindar, in the beginning, stands by her as is evident in the following conversation:

Chandidasi: They say I have the evil eye. The litle ones die of summer heat, winter's cold, and small pox, don't they? And is it any fault of mine?

Malindar: They're doomed, these fools. Ignorant idiots, is there anyone among them who can sign his name? Is there anyone with a government job? Idiots all of them. (92)

But, when, having been annoyed by her endless complaints, he says, "How can you be a witch? Those who bury children turn into Bayens, when they are possessed not witches" (92) Chandi becomes fierce in her protest. She demands an apology from him:

Chandidasi: What's that you said? So, you call me a Bayen? Me, a Bayen? That's what you said, didn't you? So you'd say I dig up the graves and raise the dead babies? Kiss them? Suckle the dead children? How could you say it?

Malindar: I was joking. . . .

Chandidasi: What a joke to crack at the expense of a mother with a child! Take back your words, else I'll beat my head against floor till I die. (Starts beating her head against the door.) (92-93)

It is this aggressiveness in her character which, resulting mainly from her sense of helplessness, gains her a sympathetic attention of the audience. A little later, we find her exhorting her husband to avenge the injustice meted out to her or, she tells him, "before your very eyes, I'll jump before the running train with Bhagirath in my arms." (94)

In all these ways, she is not only a female counterpart of male rebel but also a sensitive being pulsating with the essential human virtues of tenderness, sympathy and compassion. Her fight for her status and identity is prompted by her inner necessity to protect the higher principles of life. In fact, hers is not a social or political resistance but human resistance to all forms of tyranny. By craving for a free life, Chandi attempts to become what Gayatri Chakraborty Spivak calls an 'Organic intellectual.'

> When the subaltern 'speaks' in order to be heard and gets into the structure of responsible (responding and being responded to) resistance, he or she is on the way to becoming an organic intellectual. (14)

But the men like Gourdas, a hypocrite and a counterpart of the urban exploitative class, afraid of losing advantages, plot against her. And at his instigation, Shashi, a close relation of Malindar, accuses Chandi of being responsible for the death of his child, Tukni whom, before Bhagirath was born, Chandi had fed, bathed and given her "a pair of silver-nickelled anklets too." (92) The description of scene of implication of Chandi is realistic:

Shashi:	What a thing to do, Chandi bou? How could you do it?
Chandidasi:	What's happened, brother-in-law?
Shashi:	Tukni, my Tukni, ah! . . . Bou! Why did you ask, 'How's Tukni' and strike her with the secret arrow at once?
Chandidasi:	Tukni . . . is . . . no more?
Shashi:	Oh, how could you do it?
Chandidasi:	Me? What did I do?
Gourdas:	(to Shashi) Didn't I tell you? Now you can see it?
Chandidasi:	What are you hinting at . . . ?
Gourdas:	I've nothing to say.
Malindar:	(mad with rage) So? It seems Shashi has an adviser now in Gourdas! When neighbour's house is on fire, would you pour kerosene over the fire instead of water?
Gourdas:	Malindar, you fight with me in vain. I'm here only to stand by Shashi and take Chandi away. . . .
Malindar:	My wife won't go with you.
Gourdas:	What?
Shashi:	She . . . won't . . . go?
Chandidasi:	(Weeping in grief and from a sense of injustice) No, no, no. Find somebody else to do it for you. (93-94)

It is interesting to note that Gourdas, the clever manipulator, taking advantage of the ignorance of the village folk, attempts to eliminate Chandi for he finds in her a threat to his existence as the defender of feudal virtues. In refusing to do the job, she has broken with precedent. Therefore, she has to pay a price for her defiance of the age old conventions. To achieve his goal, Gourdas incites Shashi, who is mad with grief, against Chandi. The tactics he uses here invariably remind us of the divide and rule principle of the colonial rulers.

However, Chandi, with an unfaltering faith in human values, does not easily give in. And what follows next in the play is fraught with irony. Frightened as he is by the unusual turn of events, Gourdas pretends repentance only to deceive her into the trap. He pleads:

> How can you say that? (In control over himself. . . .) Have

> you forgotten whose daughter you are? Your ancestry? If you do not bury them, their souls remain hovering far from their destination. . . . You are their destination, you embody the mother Ganga . . . denied your service, the dead child hangs for ever over the mother. Have mercy on us, mother, forgive us our transgressions. (94)

It only reveals further the artfulness of a clever schemer. Chandi, unaware of his wicked designs, is stirred to action. She feels pity for Shashi's predicament and decides to do the last rites of his child. She majestically declares: "Go, I'll come. And let the community know that this will be the last time that I'll be on the job." (95)

What is most important to notice is that Chandi's decision is motivated more by an innate sense of sympathy for the fellow-sufferers than by the flattering words of Shashi: "There's none placed above you in our community." (94) And the motherly love in her is aroused to act when she hears the cries of the jackals in the graveyard. She leaves her suckling child to go to the cremation ground to ensure a peaceful sleep to the dead Tukni in the grave.

> (Bends over the newly dug grave. With great affection) There's nothing to be scared of, Tukni dear. I've loved you, little mother of mine, from before the time I had Bhagirath in my womb. (Caresses the grave.) It's me on guard, little mother. You needn't get a scare. I've planted throny bushes all around you, you can be sure. (95-96)

It is this human action which proves to be a threat to her very existence. The act of victimization is in the offing. The stage is set for the inevitable—an inevitable confrontation of Chandi with the degenerated social forces. Unaware of her surroundings, she goes on with her work till she is trapped and a release from which seems impossible.

The play, *Bayen*, in the main, is about the people with beliefs in superstitions and black magic and whose intellect is blunted by their insatiable greed for power and wealth and sadistic temperament. Having been the child of outmoded conventions, Chandi has become unwittingly a part of them. She has not enough courage to denounce them. In the subconscious of her mind, there is still a part which struggles to shake itself off the haunting memories of her great ancestors who symbolize the victims of discriminatory and unethical values of the feudal society. The conflict that goes on in her mind is externalized. In her long soliloquy, Chandi pours out her inner agony. An example can be seen in the following lines:

> (Shakes off her sleep and breaks into laughter to the consternation of the villagers who look at one another). O holy mother! There's no one here. What am I dreaming of sitting here all by myself? . . . They're all scared of me. (In sleepy drawl) But why I get a scare today, Gangaputta? Why this fear of a curse that would befall me because I've defied my forefathers and refused to carry on with their profession? I never had such a fear. But today . . . there's the greater fear. . . . God won't let me see you and Bhagirath ever again; Why don't you come closer to me, Gangaputta? (Wakes up with a jolt and laughs) What a rubbish really! There's none here but me! Tukni there under the banyan tree, and me on guard . . . and all the dreams.

Thus, oblivious to the danger lurking in the darkness, Chandi is lost in the humanitarian act of guarding the dead souls. And it is about this time that Gourdas sets the credulous folk on Chandi who "aware of their persence of the first time, rises to her feet, in panic." (96) Convinced that she is possessed by evil spirits and is the cause of their misfortunes, the people mercilessly attack her:

Chandidasi:	Who's there? Who are you?
Gourdas:	(Savage) See for yourself, Malindar, you bastard. It's your wife, the Bayen that's been killing our children. Why don't you ask her yourself? Who was she talking to? Whom was she fondling?
Malindar:	Chandi? Why did you leave your bed and come here?
Chandidasi:	I heard the jackals tugging at thorny bushes, scratching at the graves. I heard them and came out (to

Shashi with a nervous smile), for your Tukni's sake, brother-in-law.

The Mob: (awestruck, they point their fingers at her). You're a Bayen. . . . (The villagers drag her away in savage fury.) (96-98)

Chandi is pathetically defenceless when her husband becomes a party to the conspirarcy. Her alienation from the society seems total. Asked why her sari is dripping with milk and for whom the lullaby is, she pleads innocence: "I'm no Bayen. I've a suckling child, and that's why my breasts ooze milk all the time. Gangaputta you know it's true. Why don't you tell them?" (97)

In fact, in a male-dominated society woman is generally considered inferior to man. She has lost all her freedom. She must either conform to the existing morals or become mad and marginalized. As Patricia Waugh has justly pointed out: "If women speak outside [the symbolic] order they will either not to be heard or be heard as insane."[6] She, thus, becomes helpless. All the forces seem to have intrigued against her to deprive her of the status of a human being. Her cry for mercy has fallen on deaf ears. In the beginning of Scene 1, a moving spectacle of the woman condemned by the superstitious people is brilliantly evoked, as the direction reads: "She looks utterly exhausted and despondent, at the end of her tether, dragging her reluctant feet like some condemned ghost debarred entry into human society. . . . She wears a filthy red sari without the customary edgeline, her hair dishevelled." (83)

Surprisingly, Chandi, who bravely moves among the graves, driving the jackals away from the dead souls, fails to protect herself from being victimized by the people whose humanity has been made over to superstition, a form of domination of the vested interests. Towards the end of Scene 3, we find Malindar alone on the stage. He rearranges "his hair back to the way it was at the beginning of play, rearranges his dhoti too back to the earlier manner" (98) and beckons Bhagirath, who is supposed to have been witnessing, all the time, the enactment of inhuman separation of mother from a child, to acquaint him with the present condition of his mother, Chandi:

> Now I've told you everything. Your mother's been a Bayen ever since. They'd have burnt her to death if she had been a witch. But, son, a Bayen's not for killing. Kill a Bayen and their children start dying. . . . There listen, it's the Bayen singing her lullaby. (98)

With this speech of Malindar, the playwright takes us back to the present that is reality. And we are face to face with Chandi in her new role of Bayen (Witch). The entire drama of human relations has thus been brought to life when the playwright makes the important character an instrument of scenic display which is a device commonly seen in the folk drama. Mahasweta Devi, having the character narrate his own story, achieves greater theatrical economy and frees herself of the burden of composing the bridging scenes. In fact, Malindar himself, like the Sutradhar of the folk drama, provides a natural link between scenes.

Branded as a witch, Chandi's presence is considered inauspicious. The villagers are scared to face her for her looks may bring them misfortune and even death. The witch, as an evil-doer, is believed to have become "the enemy of the state, the individual, and of her own salvation."[7] And thus, she is denied an entry into the village even for daily bread. She is provided with the essential commodities once a week or a year. The inhumanity of the superstitious people, in forcing a fellow being to the level of an animal, is effectively depicted as Malindar makes a revelation about Chandi:

> They set up a hovel for her beside the railway track, every Saturday they leave a hamper of food for her at her doorstep. Once a year they give her two saris and two gaamchhas. . . . She couldn't let me out of her sight for a moment. But now she's been all alone for all these years. (98)

Condemned to lead a solitary life, Chandi is deprived of the right to motherhood. And her son, Bhagirath, is forbidden to enjoy the motherly affection. Interestingly, however much she is separated from the humanity, she is not devoid of human qualities. Her banishment serves as a catalyst which accelerates realization of the greater human values that are quite often ignored. Her heart is full of love for her little son. The lullaby she sings for her imaginary child is in no way different from that of any mother for her child:

> Come, sleep come to my bed of rags,
> My child god sleeps in my lap
> The elephants and horses at the palace gates,
> The dog Jhumra in the ashheap (83)

It is the mother in Bayen that sings the lullaby for her child. Her transformation from mother to the witch-mother not only sharpens her awareness which is a special attribute of the human beings but also serves as a means for her self-realization.

What is more surprising here is that Chandi bears no grudge against her persecutors. She learns to love whatever is human. What she is denied in real life, she tries to create through the power of her imagination. She longs for her son, Bhagirath, who was only a suckling child when she left him. Though, to some extent, she enjoys caressing the imaginary child, she is not unaware of the pain of being companionless. She ruminates:

> I don't have anybody any more, nobody. When I hadn't become a Bayen. I had everybody. (Puts down the pitcher, and rocks an imaginary child in her arms.) I used to rock him like this, suckle him, all that milk, a real flood, the milk from the breast spilt on the floor. (83)

Here, one is, undoubtedly, reminded of Mahasweta Devi's famous short story "Stanadayini" (Breast Giver).[8] Jashoda, the protagonist in the story, takes up the job of suckling the infants of others "for her daily meals, clothes on feast days and monthly pay." (260) And her husband, Kangalicharan, to keep her breast always full with milk, becomes a professional father. In the course of time, she develops a terrible cancer of breasts and loses her job. And all the people who fed on her milk desert her. For them she now "lying in the hospital is someone else, not mother." (275) Even while she is on her death bed, she looks for her 'milk sons.' Her condition, like that of Chandi, is touching when the narrator reveals:

> One must become Jashoda if one suckles the world. One has to die friendless, with no one left to put a bit of water in the mouth. Yet someone was supposed to be there at the end. Who was it? It was who? Who was it? When mortal plays god here below, she is forsaken by all and she must always die alone. (276)

The tragedy of Jashoda is the tragedy of the motherhood enjoined on a woman as a feudal virtue; but in reality it is only a means of perpetuation of the patriarchal conventions. But in Chandi's case, it is the denial of the motherhood that turns out to be a curse. In fact, the relationship between a mother and a son, which forms the core of Mahasweta Devi's plays and stories, acquires a metaphysical dimension, as both the mother and son are engaged in the pursuit of fulfilment in each other's martyrdom. As such, while Sujata in *Mother of 1084* is in search of her son Brati—a missing part of her soul, Bhagirath, in *Bayen*, sets out to learn of his mother, Chandi, the victim of decadent social conventions. Consider the following lines:

Bhagirath: Father?
Malindar: Yes? . . .
Bhagirath: Father, you . . . you spoke to the Bayen?
Malindar: So what, son?
Bhagirath: Isn't the living man who speaks to the Bayen doomed to die? My second mother tells me, Bhagirath come back straight from school, run whenever you hear the canister clanging otherwise she'll suck life blood. And you spoke to her? Won't she kill you off?
Malindar: No, dear, she won't kill me . . . she's a Bayen now, . . . She's your mother.
Bhagirath: My mother? The Bayen's my mother? What sort of a mother?
Malindar: You were born of her womb, my son . . . she showed you the world, she suckled you, and then she become a Bayen.
Bhagirath: But why did she become one?
Malindar: . . . She's no longer human?

Bhagirath: My mother? Without clothes? Without food? Without oil on her hair? (86-87)

Having, thus, known that Bayen is his mother, Bhagirath, the school-going child makes frequent visits to her hovel. The natural relationship between a mother and her son, which has been severed by the society is again established. A sentimental situation is created in Scene 4, when Bhagirath confronts his mother, Bayen, for the first time. Initially, Bhagirath decides not to look at her face, "I'll just see her face on the water. There can be no harm if I don't look on her face. I'll look at the shadow upon the water. The other day I didn't." (99) But he cannot restrain his inner urge to have a look at his mother as is evident in the direction: "She is about to turn around. Bhagirath notices the shadow in the water wavering. He raises his face, and for one long second they stare into each other's faces, before the Bayen turns her face away. Bhagirath stares on." (100)

Like his legendary counterpart, who, with his arduous penance, brought the sacred waters of the river Ganga down to mortal world, Bhagirath, having undergone enough penance in terms of his loss of motherly love, has crossed over the conventional boundaries to bring his mother, Chandi, the embodiment of "mother Ganga" back to society.

But Chandi fears the confrontation more than her son for she thinks that "there's a poison in the air into which I breathe, there's poison in my touch." (99) Shocked by his rhetorical enquiries—"Don't you have another sari? . . . Would you like to have a whole sari, not in shreds? Want my dhoti?" (99) and "Why do you cry?" (100) she forbids his coming there:

> Oh, my God! what do I do now? (Her voice chokes with sobs.) What do I do? (She wipes her tears away, takes a deep breath, hardens herself to speak with greater firmness) The Gangaputta's son should never again come to the trackside in the evening. I promise I won't cry again. . . . Let him go home swear that he'd never come here again to look even upon the Bayen's shadow. (100)

Chandi shudders with the realization that it is mother in her who is awake and speaks all the time to Bhagirath. She blames Malindar for not keeping an eye on the son.

The restoration of values in society which is full of the plunderers of humanity is an uphill task. Nevertheless, the natural commitment that binds a mother and her child together is impossible to be ignored by any human institution for long. And the sacrifice on the part of the victims of oppression is inevitable to defend their inalienable rights as members of the human family.[9] Thus, Chandi is seen again in action. Having seen Gourdas and his gang spread the bamboo poles on the track to stop and loot the train, she rushes to the spot and gets killed averting the accident. This act of martyrdom pulls down all the superstitions, prejudices woven around her as a bayen. Her alienation which produced an air of unreality and hence unconcern collapses under the weight of her supreme human sacrifice. She is vindicated as mother and human being . Her act of sacrifice not only exposes the exploitative system but creates a sense of urgency to end it. And it is the nature of this transformation that Chandi undergoes which adds to the dramatic interest of the play.

Chandi's heroic death is in itself an act of protest against the inhumanity of the superstition as well as inequitous social order. It is an affirmation of the undying springs of human love. And Bhagirath's defiance of the age old societal morals takes a concrete shape as he comes to acknowledge the dead as his mother:

> Let me tell you all. You can write down. . . . She's my mother. . . . Yes, sir. (The guard takes it all down.) . . . My mother (Pauses for a while, then very distinctly) . . . my mother, the late Gangadasi Chandidasi. . . . Not a Bayen. She was never a Bayen, my mother. (103)

It also enriches the play thematically insofar as it develops the theme from that of a woman to that of a human being itself.

NOTES

1. Samik Bandyopadhyay, Foreword, *Five Plays,* by Mahasweta Devi (Calcutta: Seagull Books, 1986), p. 167.
2. E. Satyanarayana, "Mothers in Mahasweta Devi's Plays: *Mother of 1084* and *Bayen*," Kakatiya Journal of English Studies, Vol. XIII (1993), p. 145.
3. Gita Aravamudan, "Traps of Tradition," *The Hindu* (Sunday) 1993.
4. Mahasweta Devi quoted in Gayatri Chakraborty Spivak, "Notes for Anvesh/Subaltern Studies Conference," p. 10.
5. N. Venugopal, "In Wright Earnest," *Indian Express*, October 13, 1991.
6. Qtd. Valerie Sutherland, "Postmodernist Strategies in Janet Frame's Scented Gardens for the Blind," *The Commonwealth Review*, Vol. III, No. 1, 1991-92, p. 124.
7. "Witchcraft," *Dictionary of the History of Ideas*, ed. Philip P. Wiener (New York: Charles Scribner's, 1973), IV, p. 521.
8. Mahasweta Devi, "Stanadayini" (Breast Giver), trans. Spivak, *Subaltern Studies*, V, pp. 252-76.
9. Satyanarayana, p. 145.

Water: Bhagirath Wins the Battle

Water, the last play in the anthology, *Five Plays*, appeared in Bengali as 'Jawl,' a short story before Mahasweta Devi made it into a play along with other stories during her second phase of playwriting in 1976-77. Like in *Aajir* and *Bayen,* Mahasweta Devi deliberately deals in *Water* with the rural life and exposes powerfully man's inhumanity to man, as she is aware that the persecution of the innocent folk continues unabated in the rural areas with an implicit acquiescence of the ruling class. The play, however, is concerned with what she calls "the history of the present"[1] and in its impulse of social protest, it is complementary to the plays discussed in the foregoing pages, but more powerful for its scathing expose of the utter indifference of the people in power towards the suffering humanity in the rural world. In fact, the area of attack is much more defined and precise than in her other plays. The play, thus, represents Mahasweta Devi's more powerful indictment of the existing social values and her unfailing commitment and passion for the underdog.

In the earlier plays, *Aajir* and *Bayen*. Mahasweta Devi attempts to show how the rural people, illiterate and ignorant, have been led into the traps laid by the vested interests. As already mentioned, a considerable part of Indian rural life, even after five decades of freedom and establishment of the so-called welfare society and its avowed commitment to the cause of the downtrodden, still experiences the trauma of inhuman subjugation at the hands of the feudal lords who really rule the roost in the villages.

The dramatic world of Mahasweta Devi is solely concerned with men and women who "moulded, groomed, trained and matured by a whole community, through and within its experience of suffering" (x) begin to defy the traditionally defined class roles and become martyrs in pursuit of their self which they value more than anything else. Samik Bandyopadhyay justly states that there is a continuum between Mahasweta Devi's "Mothers and leaders of men, between the cold, growing awareness of the former shaping into resistance, or stopping at the very edge of defiance, and the evolving militancy of the latter." (x)

Her protagonists, initially apolitical, but strongest ties binding them to community, grow to the role leader of the masses, as they absorb into their felt, personal awareness the huge impersonal, dehumanizing experience of exploitation that their community endures. In a sense, they are human in an inhuman society. And, being conscious of their inner urge for freedom, they make no bones about their hatred for the constraining conventions of the present society.

As such, the plays, except for *Mother of 1084, Urvashi O Johnny, Aajir* and *Bayen*—which are evidently devoted to expose the seedy side of the life of the urban and rural oppressed classes—have as their protagonists the beggars and archetypal outcastes, who fight a relentless battle in defence of their right to freedom and happiness.

Water is essentially a social drama in which Mahasweta Devi not only attempts, like in the preceding plays, to give an artistic expression to the age-old sufferings of the weak and the poor at the hands of the privileged but also touches on the topical issues such as Naxalite activities and their impact on the life of the rural folk.

Thus, the play, set in the rural Bengal, provides us with an authentic account of the transformation of a subaltern from a traditional water-diviner to the position of a leader of the masses, breaking down all those conventional boundaries which have been devised only to deprive his class of its human dignity.

Maghai Dome, the protagonist in the play, is a traditional water-diviner. He is an untouchable. The untouchables of the village are not allowed to draw water from the public wells, even though they are dug with Maghai's help. Santosh Pujari, an archetypal exploiter, is a power in the land. He makes the innocent folk suffer for no fault of theirs. He denies what is due to them. Trading in the relief funds meant for the poorer sections, he creates an artificial famine. The villagers, with help coming from nowhere, accept whatever little amount he fixes for their toil at his fields. Dhura, taking part in the Naxalite activities, strives hard to make his community aware that Santosh is the cause for their dehumanizing existence while his father, Maghai continues to work for him.

Jiten Maiti, an idealistic teacher, comes to their rescue. He lives with them and shares their joys and sorrows. Having sensed danger from his activities, Santosh turns the authorities against him. When he finds him difficult to deal with, he tries to bribe. But the teacher, being a staunch follower of Gandhian ideals, does not care for his personal pleasures. He continues to search for the ways to solve the problem of water caused by Santosh.

Realizing his own significance as water-diviner, Maghai becomes defiant. He pays heed to the teacher who advises him to build a dam across the river Charsa which runs by his hut: "every monsoon she overflows her banks, yet it never struck me with that this river could give us water, in days of drought." (157-58) However, Santosh, and his caste brethren, threatened as they are by the adventure of Maghai, have the authorities believe that all the outcastes have turned Naxals and Jiten is the main instigator. Thus, the play comes to an end with the authorities breaking the dam and killing Maghai who is later seen being swept away by the waters of Charsa, his beloved!

As compared to the earlier plays, *Water* is a fairly long play with a tautly-knit structure. It consists of 14 scenes in all, one of them has less than ten lines of acting part (scene 12). Mahasweta Devi has not employed any kind of technique to clog the play, though it appears to have the traces of the earlier naturalistic structure. As usual, the stage is free from the burden of all the external trappings of a conventional theatre. As already indicated, the bare stage gives the playwright more freedom to present, on the same setting, various dramatic situations that take place at different locales without taxing the belief of the audience. It also allows the playwright to be more faithful in her depiction of everyday realities of the contemporary society. And the scenes, connected logically with one another, follow in quick succession, creating an atmosphere of hectic activity which is one of the play's distinguishing features.

Besides, the influence of Brecht is clearly discernible in the incorporation of songs as well as in the tight construction of the scenes. Apparently, the playwright, by allowing her characters, at times, to address the audience directly, never lets the latter forget that it is sitting in a theatre. What is important here is that the play, for its success on the stage, relies more on the auditory and lighting effects. The effects produced through lighting and other devices at different times serve two purposes—they provide the playwright with a substitute for the unnecessary scenic displays and help the audience understand the mood of the characters on the stage. The dramatic resources of gesture and mime are used to a greater advantage. The end of each scene is suggested by the drop of curtain.

Maghai Dome, the central figure in *Water*, like Paatan in *Aajir* and Chandidasi in *Bayen*, belongs to a section of the society which has been marginalized and exploited from ancient times. In fact, by writing a play again with rural Bengal as its setting, the dramatist aims at laying bare the realities hidden from our gaze and which we never like to care for.

Maghai Dome's job is to spot the water resources whenever a new well is to be dug. Having been compelled to follow the tradition started by his ancestors, he is caught in a predicament like that of Paatan and Chandi in the preceding plays. However, unlike them, he is not bound to any external force. He is rather revered by all the people of his village for his extraordinary skills of water divining for which he claims a mythical-traditional sanction as Bhagirath of the nether Ganga. He feels proud of having inherited the secret knowledge from his great ancestors. He tells his son Dhura:

> So the nether Ganga flowed into the secret depths of mother Earth. My earliest ancestor had come all prepared to offer puja to the holy river at her advent. But by the time he arrived, Bhagirath had already left with Ganga. . . . He was just a Dome after all, and naive and so easily fooled. So he thought I must've dreamt it all. Then from the bowels of the earth, the nether Ganga herself (raises his folded palms to his head), the mother deity of all the hidden waters, spoke: You're my chosen priest. I'm the goddess, the nether Ganga, whenever

> . . . you'll pray for water . . . I tell you where to dig. . . .
> And ever since that has been our work. (125)

Mahasweta Devi's artistry lies in her capacity to present modern problems in parallelisms of past incidents. Here in the play, as in *Bayen*, she attempts to give an altogether different interpretation to the myths which the people's consciousness is steeped in and responsive to and evolves new myths to suit her own message. In an article entitled "Untapped Resources," Mahasweta Devi writes:

> It is essential to revive existing myths and adapt them to the present time and, following the oral tradition, create new ones as well. While I find the existing mythologies, epics and 'puranas' interesting, I use them with a new interpretation.[2]

Again, in a preface to the recent collection of her stories, she states:

> To capture the continuities between past and present held together in the folk imagination, I bring legends, mythical figures and mythical happenings into contemporary setting and make an ironic use of those. (xiii-xiv)

Maghai and his low-caste brethren are forbidden to draw water even from the wells meant for them. Subjected to the horrors of caste-discrimination, a large part of rural life in India is reduced to a sub-human level. The people, particularly in West Bengal, have been constant victims of both natural and man-induced famines. Caught in such excruciating situations, they either flee the villages or die of hunger. And the corrupt officials, joining hands with the privileged, seem to rub salt into the wounds of the innocent victims. It is revealed to us very early in the play (Scene 1) when Dhura is engaged in the conversation with the three Naxals:

Dhura: Strange, you're leaving, and it hurts. But Santosh Pujari? That's real devil. Always after me, pestering me with: Dhura? Why do you go to the sandbars of the Charsa river? Tell me? The bastard's dying of panic beaming his torch all around throughout the night.

Three: A real evil one, eh?

Dhura: Right. There's nothing he'll stop at. He goes to the town, collects money for relief and wouldn't spend a paisa for the stricken villages itself. Look at his house, rising from height to height. There are twenty villages bound to him in debt for ever. He'll leave nobody in peace.

Three: Water's your greatest problem, isn't that so?

Dhura: We don't know what water is. . . . My father . . . Maghai Dome, knows all about water. Every year he spots the place and Santosh digs, and there's a new well.

Three: Then what's the problem?

Dhura: They wouldn't allow us to touch it. (107)

It is the water which the play appears to be all about acquires a metaphysical dimension, when the search for it results in an unavoidable conflict between the oppressed and the oppressor and eventual defeat of the latter.

The first scene indeed demonstrates all the remarkable features of Mahasweta Devi as a dramatist. As a well-executed exposition, it not only introduces us to the major characters in the play—Mahgai Dome, Dhura and Santosh Pujari—but also hints at the central conflict: "My father . . . knows all about water. . . . They wouldn't allow us to touch it"—giving up wholly the tricks that some indulge in endowing different characters with distinguishing twists and turns of speech, the playwright allows Dhura to state the central theme, in as few words as possible, which in fact creates an atmosphere of urgency and forces the audience to respond intellectually to the plight of the character on the stage. And with this open statement of Dhura, the action of the play moves swiftly, revealing to us a number of other dramatic situations which mark the progress of the play.

Struck by consecutive draughts, the life of the rustics becomes miserable and they turn for help to Santosh Babu who, like Gourdas in *Bayen*, is a dissembler and a typical exploiter. He is an orthodox Brahmin by caste, and for him, "the shadow of a Dome pollutes his pitcher and he'd throw away the water." (12) In fact, he wields power in the villages and even the authorities stand in awe of him. He gets a large amount of relief material from the government and hoards it to create an artificial famine so that the innocent folk obey his dictates. He does not allow the outcastes to draw water even from the panchayat wells for "we worship our gods in our houses and you eat pigs and fowl . . . isn't the water polluted if you touch it?" (117) Although he has a greater respect for Maghai and always takes his help for digging the new wells, Santosh denies him water too.

Surprisingly, Maghai, though aware of the cause of all his misfortunes, continues to work for Santosh. He knows that it is he "who's been the water-diviner for all your wells—the panchayat ones as well as the others." (117) Yet he is not able to give a drop of water to his "mothers, sons, fathers, brothers." (157) Furthermore, Maghai and his community, denied at least a meal a day, lead a dog's life. We are given an insight into the life of the subject humanity in Scene 4:

Maghai: (raising the basket close to his eyes) Can you tell me, wife, how I lost my eyesight? . . .

Phulmani: Why? What's wrong with your eyes? . . .

Maghai: I'm not weaving any patched quilt. It's only baskets I'm weaving from bamboo stalk, but even that I can't see.

Dhura: Haven't I asked you so many times to go to the town to have a check-up at the hospital, and have you ever paid heed?

Maghai: Have a check up at the hospital! Easy to say, but who pays for my going and coming back?

Dhura: Why? Santosh Pujari?

Maghai: (in rage) Hey, hey Dhura!

Dhura: (angry) He can't have a well dug without your help. So you go about helping him dig all those wells. Then why shouldn't he pay you to have your eyes treated? (120)

This passage powerfully focusses the pathos of a man who, in spite of his significant social role—"He can't have a well dug without your help"—couldn't afford to go to the town for a health check-up.

The play is noted for the conflict it presents which is essential to theatre. Maghai Dome is torn within by the conflict between his personal self and social self. And as a responsible member of his community, he always stands by his people and speaks for their rights. He does not hesitate to ask Santosh who is scared by the villagers, to distribute the relief material and dig a new well for the outcastes:

First villager: That's not for us to say, Maghai, you speak for us.
Maghai: I shall. (Sighs.) Not that it'll serve any purpose still I shall. . . .
Santosh: What's the matter?. . . .
Maghai: . . . You've collected already the government relief meant for us. Why haven't we got the money and materials yet?
Santosh: You will, you will, Maghai.
Maghai: But when? Don't you know Maatang's sister and her child have died of starvation? (115-16)

However, this enthusiasm of Maghai does not last long. The impact of the feudal values on his consciousness is so effective that he cannot think of a life other than the one he is doomed to live. Thus, Maghai, though alive to pains of the abject poverty and oppression, never tries to rebel against the society. Rather, he firmly believes that he is fated to starve. It is evident from the following dialogue.

Maghai: The one thing that's most dreadfully real is the hunger. . . . There's nothing more real than hunger.
Dhura: (softly, in pain) Father!
Maghai: Yes?
Dhura: But have you ever had a full stomach? We've never had a full stomach, neither you nor me nor mother. . . . All the paddy, all the lentils that Charsa grows, and Santosh's barns bursting with paddy, and piles of molasses and mustard seeds, and what not?
Maghai: (shaking his head) They're not for us, son. (122)

This is the voice of an old man who has become helpless in the face of elaborate exploitative mechanism in the modern society.

There is also a conflict between Maghai and his family on the one hand, and between his community and the establishment represented by Santosh, on the other. Dhura, the only son of Maghai, like Brati Chatterjee in *Mother of 1084*, is a man of ideals. He is quick to anger and "has the scorpion's doggedness." (143) He is frank, outspoken and earnest. Unlike his father, he does not mince words. He has been endowed with essential human qualities. He violently protests against whatever passes for the establishment. Influenced by the Naxalite activities, he wants to do away with the system that has subjected his community to the unmerited tortures and humiliations. He becomes restless and never hesitates to speak out what he feels is right. He is highly critical of his father's lassitude and turns down his doctrine of fatalism:

> What a shame, it's for us to burn our hearts to cinders to divine water, then to raise it from the bowels of the earth, and then they'd refuse us a drop of water, not a drop for the Domes and Chandals. I spit upon fate if that's our fate. (124)

It is the tone of a young soul vibrating with the passion of a creature that can express itself only in impulsive actions.

The distinguishing feature of *Water* is its characters. Surprisingly, for the first time, a large number of characters, about six, are handled effectively and each of them has been given ample acting part to grow into a rounded personality.

As such, Phulmani, Maghai Dome's wife, calls for critical attention. As a character, she is given an edge over other characters in the earlier plays. Although she, like Sujata Chatterjee in *Mother of 1084* and Chandidasi in *Bayen*, is both a loving mother and a sensitive wife, she is more aggressive and outspoken. We confront a typically Indian mother in her when the playwright creates a sentimental situation in Scene 4. Consider the following conversation:

Maghai: I help him dig wells? . . . Take back your words. . .
Phulmani: (continuing with her work, calmly) He's not a young

one any longer. If he'd got married, you'd have had a grandchild to hold in your lap. And what he said is the truth after all.

Dhura: You tell him that, mother!

Phulmani: (now angry) No, Dhura! A son doesn't talk to his father in that tone, shame on you (spits on the ground). It's your father's standing that gives you your standing . . . and brings us honour. Keep that in mind.

Dhura: But why? Why does father have to act the water-diviner for Santosh whenever he asks him to? . . . Tell me that.

Phulmani: You're right.

Dhura: Then?

Phulmani: But he's a Brahman by caste. Isn't he? (120-21)

As an ideal wife, she is sympathetic towards her husband. She takes on the responsibility of feeding the family. But at the same time, she misses no opportunity to point out his failure in keeping the family up. In reality, she has no illusions about the grand tradition which her husband takes pride in. The only thing she is intensely aware of is the reality of her penurious background. Thus, she is quite sarcastic when she makes a revelation about Maghai's lineage:

> The legend. Haven't you heard it ever? . . . Your father is the reincarnation of the legendary Bhagirath who brought the holy Ganga down from the heavens? . . . Your father inherited it from his father. A Dome! And then he lived the same life all through—a naked beggar kicked around by the upper castes. Now it's your turn. (123)

Phulmani is equally dauntless and outspoken when she confronts Santosh, "the government's favourite son-in-law." (13) Knowing that Santosh has already got the relief materials meant for them she exhorts him to sink a well for "we die without water, our little ones go thirsty, our women dig at the sands of the river for a cupful of water." (117) And she boldly asks him not to play tricks on the poor. She says:

> I've seen you as a kid. You can't scare me. (She points at

> Maghai.) This husband of mine is a water-diviner, he worships the water, draws out the hidden water. But I've never sung to his tune. Men trade in paddy, you trade in relief. . . . These two hands of mine are full of sores, Santosh, all from scratching about the sands of the Charsa for water. . . This year we demand a well for our use. (116-17)

It is a pathetic cry of a mother who has been through the horrors of perpetual poverty and oppression. Here her anger, which in fact results from her sense of insecurity and helplessness, is directed more against herself than against Santosh for she feels inwardly that it is the passivity and inarticulateness of her husband that bring all the trouble on the family. But the words, "I've seen you as a kid" and "I've never sung to his tune," though sounding ridiculous, undoubtedly reflect her individuality.

Dhura, like Brati, is disillusioned with the existing social system. He makes friends with the "three Naxalite babus" whom the "cops caught . . . at the Bankra Sadar station and killed them off. That's another reason for Santosh to refuse us water." (143-44) Naturally, Phulmani is concerned about Dhura for she has "lost four. You are the only one that's survived." (124) She loves him more than anything else. She wants to get him married since "at his age all Domes are fathers of children." (134)

Mahasweta Devi does not seem to focus our attention on one aspect of reality, but is interested in presenting life in its continuity, and in its fluidity. As the play unfolds itself, we get an opportunity to witness the life lived beyond the mainstream world. When Jiten, the teacher, is in favour of Dhura's principle that he "must earn a lot of money first, must have the means to feed his wife twice a day on rice" (134) before marriage, Phulmani explains:

> No, teacher. You won't understand. It's so difficult between you and us. . . . Our bodies are made for hard work. We need daughters-in-law, we need grandchildren, we need a house full of people. And it's only then that there are all those working hands. And water's easier to get. (134)

It is this philosophy of survival which, by implication, serves as a unifying force in bringing all the "working hands" together to defy all the institutions that have relegated them to the sub-human level.

In all these ways, Phulmani is a representative voice of the working class women typical of Mahasweta Devi's dramatic vision. Though she, unlike Sujata and Chandi, is not a central figure, she is very much at the centre of human drama. Following and sharing all the joys and sufferings of the protagonist, she contributes to the action of the play. In other words, Phulmani symbolizes the protagonist's other-self which struggles hard to free itself from the dead weight of the conventions thrust on him by the feudal society. And the constant complaining by Dhura and Phulmani furthers Maghai's realization of his own being as well as of the need for revolt to defend his right to freedom and happiness.

Mahasweta Devi's handling of the element of irony in *Water* is effective. She uses irony as a device to make her themes poignant and to bring them into a sharper critical focus. Maghai Dome is a progeny of the legendary Bhagirath who, with his austerities, induced Shiva to allow the sacred river to descend to the mortal world for the purpose of restoring his ancestors to life, but he is condemned to pour sand on the burning pyre of his child for he "had no water to wash it down." (123)

Unlike his predecessors, Maghai is well aware of his social status. There is nothing that can oblige him to do which he dislikes. In fact, he has the choice to act or not to act the water diviner. All the same, he opts to go on with his work of water divining for, he says, "How can I refuse to come for a job that's been handed down to me by ancestors a job that I owe to my caste" (130) and "I'll be doomed to hell if I betray that trust. I do my job and go without water." (144) So it is this awareness of filial responsibility which spurs Maghai on to his willing submission to Santosh who grabs all the water and "draws the relief . . . a lion's share out of it for himself, gives the rest to his brother-in-law, and then there's nothing for anybody else." (126-27)

What is interesting to notice is that Maghai is an ardent worshipper of nature. He has an instinctive understanding of it. Being an old lover of the river Charsa, he always takes refuge in her lap and flirts with her. He feels overjoyed when he finds her in spate. The love and hate relationship between Maghai, the old water-diviner and the whore of river Charsa is brilliantly evoked in Scene 7, when Maghai is found talking to the river.

Maghai: Ah, ah, ah, it's the fortnight of the new moon in July, with the days as dark as the nights. And . . . how beautiful you appear, my Charsa! Yes, my girl, go dancing all the way, dance, dance, dance, ah, my darling life blood! . . .

Phulmani: Just what I had thought! . . . You sit here flirting with that whore?

Maghai: What whore? Charsa? . . . such a beautiful wench, in the monsoons of June and July she breaks across the banks, she laughs with the bursts of the flood, Charsa the youthful river, and you dare to call her a whore?

Phulmani: Are you drunk or what?

Maghai: I'm drunk, not with booze, but with water. At the sight of water I get flushed, with my blood beating the madal. . . . Dhura's mother is right. You're a whore, a fallen woman. In the summer months when I scrape at your breasts, how flirt with me! (139-41)

It is this total commitment to nature which distinguishes Maghai from all those who, in the name of science, attempt to destroy it.

Ironically Maghai, in spite of his preoccupation with nature, does not make out the tidings it keeps sending all along. Spending a whole life brooding away on water, he has no time to think of anything else. He fails to reap the fruits of his knowledge of water-divining and indirectly adds to the problems of his own community. No doubt, at times, being acutely aware of his own pathetic existence, he begins to ask: "with all that water, heaps of it why do we go without water?" (144) But he does nothing to realize his dream of having plenty of water. In fact, he is not bold enough to defy Santosh that is the establishment. He is a creature to be pitied. Though apparently it is a sense of duty that inspires him to work for Santosh, Maghai fears him for more reasons than one. When Jiten asks him why he is scared of Santosh, he reveals:

> You won't understand. He's the landowner of landowners, the money-lender of money-lenders. The SDO and the police chief go by his brief, they send relief through him. Oh God, there are times I have a vision of a dawn, with Santosh rising in the East, turning the sky a blazing red and pouring sheets of fire. (142)

Here the playwright tries to bring home to us the extent to which the powerful exploitative system has spread creating smothering effects on the psyche of the rural folk.

Moved by the precarious condition of the outcastes, Jiten an ideal teacher and "follower of Gandhi . . . served a term in jail during the August rebellion in 1942, and he wouldn't claim the pension . . . never run for personal gain . . . even the SDO rises to his feet when he calls on him" (133) devotes himself to find out the ways to release them from all kinds of traditional traps. He lives with the Domes and teaches their children. His identification with them is complete as he fights for their rights.

Surprised though he is, Jiten suggests that there must be science behind Maghai's mysterious water-divining skills and always defends him. When an officer, out of anger, calls Maghai "an illiterate fool" and his act "Mumbo-jumbo," Jiten flies into a rage:

> Our country's exceptional, don't you realize that? Knowledge and culture here have nothing to do with literacy as such. Someone like Maghai can have both knowledge and culture. They'd have a mind like a continent that no one has cared to explore. (132)

Here it is the alter-ego of the playwright that speaks. The words "knowledge and culture here have nothing to do with literacy as such" invariably remind us of Mahasweta Devi's comment regarding the superstitions of the tribal people:

> I don't like to call them superstitious. They have their own culture and tradition and they are inferior to none. Actually, they are more cultured than the men in the mainstream society.[3] (my translation)

But a good man like Jiten meant a lot to the innocent people. By attempting to enlighten and bring reality to the community conscience, he earns the wrath of Santosh who can't stand a good man. In fact, Santosh has already complained to the SDO about Jiten who visits "the settlements of the Domes and Chandals, that you tell them drinking's bad . . . you eat pork with them you've saved Parash's son . . . in May you took the lead in fighting the fire when the Dusad settlements went up in flames." (143)

The action of Scene 8 takes place in the town in the chamber of the SDO. We find Jiten and the SDO sitting face to face. He has come here to inform the latter about the plight of people of Charsa. But the SDO seems to care a fig for all that Jiten tells him. We are provided with an opportunity to see how the indifferent bureaucrats singing to the tune of the privileged, aggravate the sense of insecurity and alienation among the downtrodden when Jiten takes the SDO to the task for neglecting his duties:

SDO: What were you saying?
Jiten: I've told you everything already.
SDO: Nonsense.
Jiten: Nonsense? What do you mean?
SDO: Don't tell me of new problems, please don't. As it is, the district has a load of problems already. Drought followed by drought, flood followed by flood . . . chronic! Problems stick to this district like incurable dysentery. Charsa's only a block in the district, and has regular supply of relief. A lot of cash too!
Jiten: Not the block, it's Santosh who gets it all . . .
SDO: I know all about that, but it's for the BDO to see to it, It's such a shaky system!
Jiten: There's more to it, there's caste discrimination. Santosh doesn't let the Domes have water.
SDO: No, there isn't.
Jiten: Are you sure?
SDO: Officially speaking, there isn't. . . . Unofficially speaking I'll admit, it's there. It's there in the blood of the people . . . how can you get rid of it? (145-46)

In the corrupt ethos of modern society, no doubt, the SDO's attitude has its appealing honesty and can be seen as realistic. But we learn towards the end of the scene, that the SDO himself is a party to the atrocities perpetrated on the untouchables and his hard-headed realism is only a device to cover his degenerated soul.

About this time, Santosh who is supposed to be eavesdropping, comes in and asks the teacher not to set the SDO on him. He asks him "to make a deal. From the next relief grant let's split sixty-forty, big amount for you!" (147) Jiten is nonplussed. He threatens Santosh with severe consequences when he says again: "well, if you won't have a share of the relief grants, why don't you take a bicycle?" (148) Frightened by the unusual turn of the situation, the SDO intervenes and Santosh leaves saying: "I meant well but he took it all wrong." (148) Jiten squarely blames the SDO for all the troubles of the people of Charsa. "With officers like you," he says, "Santosh carries on with his mischief. It's your inaction that supports Santosh." (148) We come to know, for the first time, that Santosh is "a dirty man. He was beaten up twice at the Charsa station. Once for selling illicit liquor. The other time for molesting a coolie girl. Twice arrested, twice released." (148) The scene ends with the SDO and Santosh planning to build "a temple for the village goddess Maa" (149) instead of a well for the untouchables. Evidently, something is to come out of this.

What impresses one about Santosh is his paradoxical character. He is mean, hypocritical and a ruthless exploiter of the innocent people, but all through he is true to himself. Though he wants to get rid of Jiten and Maghai, he has a high opinion about both of them. When the SDO assures him of the help from the Geological Survey to dig wells, Santosh mockingly says: "A fat lot of good they'll do. They'll only bring machines, drill the earth, blast the rocks. Maghai can beat them hollow, with nothing of that." (160) All the same, he complains to the authorities about Maghai and plans to kill him. But he suffers from the pricks of conscience! He could not help admitting his gratitude to Maghai. Thus, filled with remorse, he confesses:

> What a sinner I am, what a great sinner, now I have to harm this learned man. It hurts me here: I grew up rocking in a

> cradle that Maghai made. He used to make wonderful bird-snares for me. Oh! what a shame! (160)

The contradictory personality of Santosh is revealed further when he thinks of making Jiten and Maghai happy in Scene 12. He tells his servants:

Santosh:	Maghai wanted to buy a palmyra stalk. Go and give him two of them for free.
1st Servant:	Ok, sir.
Santosh:	Carry two brimful baskets of the prasad from the Shitala puja for Maghai and Jiten.
2nd Servant:	Ok, sir.
Santosh:	I'll pay to repair the school building. . . . What remorse! What misery! Why did Jiten have to come here? Why? (160)

The irony underlying the passage is all the more striking as we recall an earlier conversation between Maghai and Jiten in Scene 7.

Jiten:	No, no, that can't be true. He sends me prasad after the pujas so often.
Maghai:	Haven't you noticed how the householder fattens the sacrificial goat? (143)

Scene 9 takes us back to the village. Maghai and Dhura are seen walking along "the dry bed of the Charsa. Dhura has a bow and arrows in his hand." (150) While Maghai enjoys the beauty of nature, Dhura is seized with a desire to kill Santosh. In fact, being in the lap of nature, he reveals his true self. Here the spontaneous animal vigour of Dhura is balanced by tolerant and relaxed temperament of Maghai. Symbolically, they are the two selves of nature itself. So, becoming one with nature, Maghai has forgotten about his 'self.' He is kind and benevolent and always ready to work for others. He has his own mind and knows no rebellion. Thus, he becomes a willing tool in the hands of Santosh. When his son professes to finish off the latter with an arrow, Maghai, trembling with fear warns him not to mention "his name even in a joke." (150) Now Jiten joins in their conversation. Surprisingly enough, it is the other Jiten Maiti that comes into view—"business-like, practical, disciplined, the veteran leader of men—his gestures, his manner of speaking, his gait, all now marked by a dogged purpose." (151) Actually, he has come with a new proposal to solve the water problem of the Domes. Maghai is all ears as Jiten explains how the people of Charsa, by building a dam across the river, could be redeemed from the eternal curse of going without water.

Jiten: (demonstrates by drawing with a chalk on the backdrop . . .) For this half a mile, the river, when in spate, doesn't overflow its high banks . . .

Maghai: So what?

Jiten: The region abounds with boulders. If we could gather the boulders and dam the river up here, within its high banks . . .

Maghai: (his eyes have a sharper look, his body taut with excitement) Then?

Jiten: The monsoon brings rains, and blows away. But there'll be water stored within the dam after the monsoon's passed. A few boulders might be washed away, but not all of them. . . . The dam will hold water. (152)

In his deep commitment to the cause of the untouchables, Jiten undoubtedly recalls the old widow in Bharati Sarabhai's *The Well of the People* (1943). The old woman, a brahmin, wishes to go to the Kumbha Mela herself so that her husband might be salvaged in the other world. But since one of her legs is broken and she cannot afford a companion to take her to Haridwar with her petty hoard of seventy rupees, she decides to sink a well for a temple where no untouchable would be denied water. Even for this, she finds her hard earned savings inadequate and comes to a banker for a loan. In repayment, she offers to slave for the rest of her life in his house. Although the motive behind her act is quite different from that of Jiten, what both of them are concerned with is the common good of the society in which they live.

After this event, the play takes a new turn. In the protagonist,

Maghai, we see the maximum metamorphosis. The very thought of building a dam across the river boosts his morale and makes him feel superior. His happiness knows no bounds. He takes "a deep breath, moves away from Jiten, and acts out with a flourish."

> We'll start at once, teacher! I can see the dam, it's . . . real, we have built it now. We have gathered the water, we've taught the whore of the Charsa a lesson at last, she won't keep us in the throes of her bitter, dry love any more. Oh, what heaps of water! Dhura's mother draws water, Dhura and I till the land. Dhura, look at the crops, the sheer abundance of it! Now we've sown the seeds, and we bathe in the dam. (153)

It is no idle talk for, towards the end of the scene, Maghai and his men are engaged in the construction of the dam "carrying boulders dropping them in the river bed." In fact, the whole act of building a dam is evoked when the playwright makes the chorus sing:

> Hei Lanka, Hei Lanka,
> We're on the way to Lanka,
> A boulder on our backs,
> A boulder on the ground,
> We're building the bridge to Lanka.
> Hei Lanka, Hei Lanka. (153)

Another striking feature of *Water* is its poetic quality. Mahasweta Devi endows the play with a number of poetic passages and songs which make it precise not only for the actor to work but also for the audience to react to. Maghai describes Phulmani as "the late monsoon sky just before autumn. Now heavy with clouds, rent with streaks of lightning, and the next moment clear and shining and smiling." (124) Almost all the characters slide into poetry whenever they are under stress. The following passage by Phulmani is a case in point:

> Water! I've never known the joy that comes at the sight of

> water in plenty, unless it's Charsa in spate in the rainy month. Look at these leper's fingers of mine, all from digging into the sands for water. I dig and dig a shallow hole in the night, all through the night, till a little water trickles into the hole, ah! the gift of Charsa, to be gathered in before dawn breaks lest the first rays of the sun soak it up. And . . . I've never known it myself, how it feels to be free to drink as much water as you'd like to till your thirst is really quenched? (122-23)

When he performs the ritual of water-divining, Maghai bursts into singing which gives "the event a metaphoric charge."

> O mother, the nether Ganga! Why don't you pay heed to my prayers? Pay heed, O holy mother of the nether Ganga, you the preserver of life, you the nurse, you lord it over being and creation, life and death. . . .
> The water lies captive deep down,
> Till it gushes out at the Mother's bidding.
> O water, to whom do you belong?
> I belong to him who knows how to call me. (131)

The playwright, by using songs actually attempts to focus our attention on the philosophical implication of the events and characters as well.

Notwithstanding his life-long love-affair with river Charsa, Maghai fails to realize his dream—a dream to quench the thirst of all his people. But he seems to decode, for the first time, the offering of perennial water the river carries in its seasonal bounty and regrets for having misunderstood nature. He tells Phulmani:

Maghai: (desperately eager to get his feelings across to Phulmani, with the fear that his words might prove inadequate) How I abused her, wife! Called her whore, flirt, showing off her water in spate one minute, and snatching it away the next, to a dry, sandy bed.

Phulmani: (laughs, but shows that she is moved) Go on.

Maghai: Oh, how my words must have hurt her, the river! She must've thought, why should they get me wrong? She

> must've said, I can give you water, it's you who can't draw it from me. Wife, the river's a woman. In the monsoon floods, she was giving me hints every year—hints for a store of water. (158)

It is the sense of guilt in the protagonist which, apparently resulting from the awareness of his inner being, gives the play a metaphorical dimension. In fact, for Maghai, the construction of dam in itself is an act of protest and self-assertion against the retrograde conventionalities of feudal society.

Pretending to be unconcerned, Santosh says: "the dam's a good thing for everyone. . . . I don't mind, if it helps you. I wish you all luck." (154) But he could not bear to see the untouchables quench their thirst with plenty of water from "a lovely dam." He feels hurt to think that "the dam will have to be broken and all those men to be arrested." (161)

In fact, sensing a threat from a community that has learnt to control nature, a sure sign of defiance of the dominance of the present system of which he is a representative, Santosh turns the authorities against the Domes. He informs the SDO that Jiten, who is a "Mahishya by caste . . . had no business to serve the casteless" (159) has incited the Domes and Chandals into building a dam on the river. We learn from the conversation that the SDO, being deceived into the belief that Jiten is "manufacturing super guns, live ones, human ones" and "training cadres for the struggle" (162) orders the police officers to open fire at the slightest provocation during the opening ceremony of the dam.

Unaware of the impending danger, Maghai and his men gather at the dam to offer puja to Manasa, the snake goddess. The entire scene appears to have assumed the pristine innocence and beauty characteristic of the people living close to nature, as Maghai and his men indulge in fun and frolic celebrating their achievement. They sing and dance to "the dholak player till a loud, long cooee breaks in . . . coming closer and closer." (164) Suddenly, Phulmani who actually makes this sound so as to warn the revellers of the danger, enters the stage and announces: "Santosh has brought in police force. Run for your lives, all of you." (164) When told that the police are breaking the dam, Maghai becomes furious. He cannot stand his dream being shattered. He exhorts his men to go forward and "crush the bastards with pole." (164) For a while, the stage is the scene of brutal attack and resistance. The direction reads:

> The police enter with the men beating them mercilessly with the butts of their rifles. Maghai is not with them. Jiten, Dhura and some of the others try to hit back. . . . Jiten snatches a policeman's rifle from his hand and throws it away. A policeman brings down a crushing blow with the butt of his rifle on Jiten's head. Jiten falls to the ground with a wail. (165)

A moment later, we find Maghai on the stage, "tottering, one hand on his bleeding chest." (165) In his confrontation with the brutal force of Santosh, Maghai is severely wounded. But he is not to die an ordinary death because "It's the Bhagirath of the nether Ganga," he declares: "I can't let them carry me as a corpse into their bloody morgue. My last journey will be with the water." (165) So saying, Maghai falls to the ground. The play comes to an end with Maghai being carried away on the crest of rising and gushing waters of mad Charsa. Thus, the play, *Water*, brings out the Promethean nature of man in struggle against oppressive system as well as with nature.

NOTES

1. Qtd. Samik Bandyopadhyay, introduction, *Five Plays* (Calcutta: Seagull Books, 1986), p. xiii.
2. Mahasweta Devi, "Untapped Resources, " *Seminar*, 359 (July 1989), p. 17.
3. "Kondakonala Velugu Dari Mahasweta Devi," *Udayam* (Telugu) Sept. 30, 1991.

Conclusion

Although drama is not new to Indian genius and has been hailed as "Fifth Veda," Indian drama in English has not made much headway chiefly because of the lack of a living theatre and a live audience. It took a long time for drama to gain a respectable status in the field of Indian literature in English. Michael Madhusudan Dutt's *Is This Called Civilization?* the first English play, appeared in 1871. And since then, a number of plays have been written and translated into English despite the fact that drama in English attracted only the elite. Surprisingly, Indian playwrights in the pre-Independence period followed the tradition of Elizabethan drama through and through. As M.K. Naik rightly comments: "It is . . . significant that Kailasam and Sri Aurobindo invariably cast their . . . plays in the age-old Shakespearian mould, without at all pondering whether the form was still artistically viable in the modern context."[1] Furthermore, they turned to the popular myths and legends for the material of their plays. In fact, they wrote to cater to the need of the escapist theatre. However, the establishment of Indian People's Theatre Association (IPTA) by the enthusiastic artists of Bengal has given a new lease of life to realistic drama. And the new dramatists were concerned with the subjects like slum life, untouchability, exploitation of the weak and the poor and conventional morality.

The field of contemporary Indian drama boasts of only a few dramatists with a keen eye for the dramatic. A glance at the major concerns of the contemporary playwrights—Asif Currimbhoy, Girish Karnad, Vijay Tendulkar and Badal Sircar—reveal that initially they have been carried away by the themes of topical interest and existential problems of man. But as they grew into mature artists, they showed a concern for the common man. Interestingly, now this enthusiasm and commitment to the cause of suffering humanity begins to lose its vigour as most of them learn to play the market. But the modern Indian playwright who is an exception to this is Mahasweta Devi whose dramatic work is the product of her direct confrontation with the prevailing social system.

Though playwriting is not her forte, Mahasweta Devi's dramatic output deserves critical attention. She adopts this medium not only to explore the anguished consciousness of the oppressed and exploited but also to focus the indifference of the people in power towards these sections. Moreover, theatre provides her an easy access to the larger illiterate audience that is India. In an interview given to the *Seagull Theatre Quarterly,* Mahasweta Devi says, "theatre is visual it will reach more people. Most of my stories . . . have travelled far, reached (inaccessible) interior places also. . . . My only point is let it reach people. It must work."[2] And in another interview to Samik Bandyopadhyay, she states: "If I work in drama . . . I'll do it for my people.[3] This certainly explains her single-minded commitment and passion for the poor. She has been more accurate in her portrayal of the harsh realities of poverty, exploitation and death in the contemporary society. Like Arnold Wesker, she is a progressive writer. She makes avowal of her sympathies for the exploited. Even though, her theatre professedly employs realistic technique, her compassion and care for people and her desire to improve existing social condition betray her idealism. However, she should not be classified with the propagandists for she does not believe in the programme of any political party, nor is she interested in political activities as such.

In fact, the source of inspiration in all her work seems to be an anger, luminous, burning, and passionate, directed against a system that has failed to liberate the people from these horrible constraints.[4] So her protagonists in the plays rebel against existing morals and become martyrs. Mahasweta Devi appears to suggest one thing that the solution to the age-old oppression and exploitation lies in the hands of the oppressed. And sacrifice on the part of the victims is inevitable to defend their inalienable rights to freedom and happiness. In a foreword she wrote for *Rakasi Kora* in Telugu translation, she says: "When they [the oppressed] rise, get organised and fight back, only then history can be changed."[5]

What makes her dramatic world artistically significant is its simple structure. As S. Mokashi-Punekar rightly observes: "Quite often we forget that simplicity in art is quite a complex thing which has to be created after much sophisticated effort."[6] Accordingly, she avoids the claptrap of dramaturgy to achieve the simplicity. Thus, her plays are written in scenes. The devices like recorded tape, mime, gesture and chorus are used to a greater advantage. In fact, she links gestures with dialogue so that they make a more subtle impression. Her theatre like that of Badal Sircar is poor. In other words, it is free from the burden of external trappings like settings and other devices that are generally connected with commercial theatre.

Like Brecht, Mahasweta Devi never tries to disguise the stage apparatus so as to make the audience aware that it is sitting in a theatre. This helps in the establishment of a direct connection between the actors and the audience. The influence of Brecht is also discernible in her use of songs as well as in her letting the characters directly address the audience which is essential to create an antidote to the theatrical illusion. Besides, Mahasweta Devi, being familiar with the street theatre which has exerted a tremendous influence on the general audience in India, models her scenes on the street plays. Thus, the important characters in *Aajir* and *Bayen*, as in street plays, are allowed to transform in full view of the audience to enact an episode in the past. By giving a single character different roles, Mahasweta Devi has achieved greater dramatic economy.

Her masterful use of irony is perhaps her most powerful stylistic tool. In fact, the entire corpus of Mahasweta Devi's dramatic work is infused with ironic comment. In *Bayen*, the heroine is a gravedigger. She buries the dead children and guards them from the jackals. But, ironically enough, she, having been branded a witch, is separated from her suckling child and family. And in *Water*, the protagonist Maghai is a water diviner by profession. He is a progeny of Bhagirath who brought the river Ganga down to the mortal world in order to restore his ancestors to life, but he ironically, denied water, is compelled to pour sand on the burning pyre of his dead son.

Through the devices of parallel and contrast, the singleness of effect is produced in the plays. In *Mother of 1084*, Mahasweta Devi contrasts Dibyanath with Somu's father. While the former is indifferent at the news of his son's death and tries to hush up the incident, the latter, a poor and helpless man, runs from pillar to post crying his heart out for his son who is killed along with Brati in a confrontation with the supporters of the ruling party. In *Water*, the hero, Maghai, is contrasted with the learned lot from the Geological Survey of India only to focus the superiority of illiterate Maghai over the latter in the matters of divining water and understanding nature.

Mahasweta Devi powerfully employs common man's speech to bring to her theatre a realistic flavour. The ordinary language without any constraint of stage artificiality is really revolutionary in its impact. It gives the playwright an opportunity to catch the rhythm, idiom and vocabulary of the social class she writes about. Thus, her plays abound in colloquialisms, unconventional swear-words and "four letter words." As Mahasweta Devi maintains, "using dialect . . . is necessary because it enriches language."[7] Phulmani in *Water* tells when the teacher asks her whether the untouchables complained at the court against Santosh, the exploiter:

> Who'll go for that, teacher? Tell me that, Santosh is the government's favourite son-in-law. The bastard filches from the government relief. . . . The demon of demons that he is, when it comes to digging wells from the relief funds, he wouldn't take our men on for labourers. (135-36)

The language here she uses to express her emotion approximates the speech of the ordinary people in real life. Yet another example can be seen in *Mother of 1084*. When Brati's sister, Neepa, finds fault with her husband Amit's attitude towards Brati, Amit angrily says: "It was you who were ashamed of Brati. Not me. . . . I come from one of the best families around. . . . I'm not going to take that from a three-penny whore." (33)

Mahasweta Devi has taken unusual themes from contemporary life and transformed them into plays of artistic excellence. In fact, experience and factual detail are the ground on which her drama is inscribed. Survival through struggle is the central message of her dramatic creation. There is an implicit design even in the arrangement of her plays to bring home to us the different modes of exploitation and oppression of the hapless people. Thus, the plays may be conveniently divided into two groups—the rural plays and the urban plays. While *Mother of 1084* and *Urvashi O Johnny* deal with urban life, *Aajir, Bayen* and *Water* explore the realities of lowly life in the rural world.

The first play *Mother of 1084* deals with a mother who is a victim of the constraints of the male-dominated society. Sujata, the central figure, is a misfit in her own family.Though she is well aware of the corrupt degenerated values represented by her husband Dibynath, she fails to disconnect herself with them and leads a compromising life. She loves her younger son, Brati, who is a man of clear ideas, but she does not try to know about his activities. Disillusioned with the present system, Brati takes to revolutionary activities. He never lets his mother know of his true self, although he thinks high of her. As he is engaged in the programme of liberating the people from the clutches of the exploitative system, Brati is brutally killed. Ironically, Sujata comes to learn about his sacrifice only two years after his death as she visits the people with whom Brati is associated. The search for her son leads to realization of her own being as mother, woman and human being. And in the end, Sujata, having found a parallel to her own silent protest against the patriarchal system in Brati's rebellion, exhorts the people to wake up from slumber and fight for their inalienable rights.

Aajir is the story of a slave. The protagonist Paatan, coming from the family of slaves, is denied a right to love and marriage. He is not even entitled to lead an ordinary life. Unaware of the fact that the bond, which was signed by his ancestor, had long turned to dust, Paatan bears calmly all kinds of humiliation at the hands of his master. However, he comes to know of the fact through the mistress of the house who provokes him to quench her lust. Seeing in her a mother, Paatan does not yield to her. Towards the end of the play, he agrees to her proposal of elopement when she assures him of the release from eternal enslavement. In an attempt to free himself of the so-called bond, Paatan throttles the mistress to death. Surprisingly, there is no bond as such and he realizes that he is "no longer a slave and like everyone he is free."

The third play, *Urvashi O Johnny*, is apparently concerned with the urban underworld of beggars and their tribulations in the face of indifferent establishment. Johnny, an orphan, is a ventriloquist by profession. He dreams of running the mundane world into a paradise of happiness with his tricks. He treats the marionette as if it were his beloved and turns down any offer of love and marriage from his mentors. This infatuation results in a cancer of throat. In fact, he is an artist with a purpose. Being conscious of the inhuman morals of the repressive system, Johnny takes on the responsibility of enlightening the masses. He runs after the "birds of happiness." He does not care for himself. The kind doctor and his friends who are concerned about his health, warn against his obsession with the talking doll which may lead to a loss of voice completely. Johnny finds it difficult to part with his profession as it gives at least a momentary pleasure both to himself and to the audience that is people. Thus, the profession of ventriloquism becomes a life long obsession with Johnny and he continues to flirt with the marionette till the end of his life.

Bayen, the fourth play, is a moving story of a sensitive mother who, like Sujata, is placed against the powerful patriarchal institution. Chandi, the central character is a gravedigger. Her job is to bury the dead children and protect them from jackals at night. As long as she remains unmarried and is not blessed with a child, she goes on with her work without any complaint. She is fed up with her routine job. Having found an image of her baby son in the dead children she buries, Chandi pleads with her husband Malindar, to release her from the constraints thrust on her by the feudal society, by taking her to a town where nobody knows about them. Malindar pays no heed to her complaints. Rather, he asks her to continue with her job as it is a symbol of social status. However, Chandi does her work not for the material pleasures but for an obligation she has towards her ancestors. Besides, the mother in her is moved to action whenever she finds others suffer. So Chandi, in spite of herself, is involved in the work of guarding the graves at night. About this time, the gullible people led by Gourdas, a hypocrite and exploiter, brand her as a witch and condemn her to live away from her son and family. Though she is reduced to the animal status by the society, she is not devoid of human passions. In fact, the separation from her son and society has led to the realization of her being as a mother and a human being. When Gourdas plans to stop and loot the train by spreading bamboo sticks on the railways, Chandi runs to the spot and dies in an attempt to avert the accident. The defiance of age-old feudal values takes concrete shape as her son, Bhagirath comes forward to acknowledge the dead as his mother.

Water, the last play, tells a tale of an untouchable who is a water diviner. Maghai Dome, like Paatan and Chandi, is in conflict with the feudal society. Maghai and his community are denied water. Santosh Babu, the archetypal exploiter, keeping for himself a large amount of relief material meant for the poor, creates an artificial famine in the village. He does not allow the untouchables to draw water from the wells dug with the help of Maghai. Although Maghai knows well about his own skills of water divining, he fails to provide water for his people. Jiten, an ideal teacher, moved by the plight of the untouchables, dedicates himself to find the way to solve the problem of water. With his selfless service, Jiten inspires the community. They learn to realize their own identity. Jiten tells Maghai to build a dam across the river which may quench their eternal thirst. But Santosh, sensing a threat to his existence, informs the authorities that all the untouchables have turned Naxalites and the teacher is the main conspirator. Thus, Santosh along with the police break the dam, as Maghai and his men are busy with the celebration of their achievement. A long and fierce fighting ensues. Towards the end of the play, Maghai is seen being carried away on the crest of waves of furious river Charsa, his faithful beloved.

Repetition of themes, characters and situations undoubtedly tempt one to think that the dramatic vision of Mahasweta Devi is limited. But the ubiquity of oppression in society is a justification and also an argument against the charge of repetition. An appreciation of her achievement as a dramatist demands a sympathetic understanding and identification with the cause of suffering humanity. Thus, considering the themes which represent her unflinching faith in human dignity and her deft use of elements to make her plays successful on the stage, it must be admitted that Mahasweta Devi emerges as a significant playwright.

NOTES

1. M.K. Naik, "The Achievement of Indian Drama in English," *Perspectives on Indian Drama in English* (Madras: Oxford University Press, 1979), p. 185.
2. Mahasweta Devi, *The Seagull Theatre Quarterly*, Issue I (January, 1994), p. 19.
3. Qtd. Bandyopadhyay, Introduction, *Five Plays by Mahasweta Devi* (Calcutta: Seagull Books, 1986), p. xii.
4. *Ibid.*, p. ix.
5. Mahasweta Devi, Foreword, *Rakasi Kora* (trans. from Bengali into Telugu by S. Sita Ram, Hyderabad: HBT, 1982).
6. Mokashi-Punekar, "The Plays of Bharati Sarabhai," *Perspectives on Indian Drama in English* (Madras: Oxford University Press, 1977), p. 145.
7. Mahasweta Devi, "Untapped Resources," *Seminar*, 359 (July, 1989), p. 19.

Bibliography

PRIMARY SOURCES

A. SELECTED PLAYS

Devi, Mahasweta. *Five Plays: Mother of 1084, Aajir, Bayen, Urvashi O Johnny* and *Water.* Calcutta: Seagull Books, 1986.

B. NOVELS AND SHORT STORIES

Devi, Mahasweta. *Jansir Ranee.* Calcutta: New Age, 1956.

______. *Amrita Sanchay.* Calcutta: India Associated, 1962.

______. *Rakasi Kora* (Translated from Bengali by S. Sitaram). Hyderabad Book Trust, 1982.

______. *Evaridee Adavi* (Aranyer Adhikar) (Trans. from Bengali into Telugu by P. Sheshagiri Rao). HBT, 1985.

______. *Operation? Bashai Tudu.* Trans. Samik Bandyopadhyay. Calcutta: Thema, 1990. 1-148.

______. "Draupadi." *Bashai Tudu.* Trans. Samik Bandyopadhyay. Calcutta: Thema. 1990. 149-62.

______. "Seeds." *Panorma: An Anthology of Modern Indian Short Stories*, ed. Mulk Raj Anand and S. Balu Rao. New Delhi: Sterling, 1986. 20-43.

______. "Breast Giver." Trans. Gayatri Chakraborty Spivak. *Subaltern Studies.* New Delhi: Oxford University Press, 1987. 252-76.

______. *Imaginary Maps.* Trans. Gayatri Chakraborty Spivak. Calcutta: Thema, 1993.

______. "Shishu." Trans. Pinaki Bhattacharya. *Women Writing in India.* Ed. Susie Tharu and K. Lalitha. New York: Feminist Press, 1993. 236-51.

______. "Salt." *Indian Literature*, 157 Sept-Oct, 1993, pp. 99-114.

______. "Etoa Munda Won the Battle." Trans. Meenakshi Mukherjee. New Delhi: National Book Trust, 1989.

C. ARTICLES

Devi, Mahasweta. 'Untapped Resources.' *Seminar*, 359, July 1989: 15-19.

______. "Terai Udyamam." *Srujana* (Telugu) Dec.15, 1992: 19-22.

______. "Story of Chuni Kotal." *Economic Political Weekly*, Vol. XVIII, April 1993, 16-28.

______. "The Call Never Comes: Unemployment among Tribals." *Economic Political Weekly*, Vol. XVIII, 2 July 1983: 1216-17.

______. "Lodhas of West Bengal-I." *Economic Political Weekly,* Vol. XVIII, No. 22 (1983): 947-49.

______. "Lodhas of West Bengal-II," *Economic Political Weekly,* Vol. XVIII, No. 23 (June 1983): 997-98.

D. INTERVIEWS

Burgula. "Manava Sevalo Mahasweta Devi." *Udayam* (Telugu), August 4, 1991: 10.

"Girijanula Rajakeeya Chaitanyam Nunche Udyamalu Udbavisthai." *Praja Paksha Patrika* (Telugu), Sept. 16-23, 1992: 14-15.

Raju, Surendra. "Aame Kalam Aadivasula Aathmakathanam." *Suprabhtam* (Telugu), Oct. 20, 1991: 78-79.

E. PREFACE/FOREWORD

Devi, Mahasweta. Preface. *Bashai Tudu* by Mahasweta. Trans. Samik Bandyopadhyay and Gayatri Chakraborty Spivak. Calcutta: Thema, 1990: xv-xxi.

______. Foreword. *Rakasi Kora* by Mahasweta. Trans. S. Sitaram. HBT, 1982.

F. ARTICLES ON MAHASWETA DEVI

Katyal, Anjum, "The Metamorphoses of 'Rudali.'" *Seagull Theatre Quarterly,* 1 (1994): 5-11.

Mukherjee, Sujit. "Mahasweta Devi's Writings: An Evaluation." *Book Review*, Vol. XV, No. 3 (1991): 30-31.

"Rudali: Questions of Language and Audience." *Seagull Theatre Quarterly,* 1 (1994): 12-24.

"Rudali: The Making of a Production." *Ibid.*, 25-34.

Satyanarayana, E. "Mothers in Mahasweta Devi's Plays: *Mother of 1084* and Bayen." *Kakatiya Journal of English Studies,* Vol. XII (1993): 138-46.

______. "The Unconquered: A Study of Mahasweta Devi's Short Story 'Draupadi.'" *Indian Women Novelists*, ed. R.K. Dhawan. New Delhi: Prestige, 1995. Set III, Vol. 7, 177-84.

Spivak, Gayatri Chakraborty. Foreword. "Draupadi by Mahasweta Devi."

Trans. Spivak. *Writing and Sexual Difference,* ed. Elizebeth Alsel. Great Britain: Harvest Press, 1982: 261-72.

______. "Deconstructing Historiography." *In Other Worlds: Essays in Cultural Politics* by Spivak. New York: Methuen, 1987: 197-221.

______. "A Literary Representation of the Subaltern: Mahasweta Devi's 'Stanadayini.'" *Subaltern Studies*, Vol. II. New Delhi: Oxford University Press, 1987: 91-134.

______. "Notes for Anveshi/Subaltern Studies Conference" (Unpublished and shelved at Anveshi Research Centre for Women, Hyderabad).

Venugopal, N. "In Wright Earnest," *Indian Express* (Sunday Magzine), 13 Oct. 1991: 2.

G. OTHER TEXTS CONSULTED

Anand, Mulk Raj. *Untouchable.* New Delhi: Arnold Heinemann, 1981.

______. *Coolie.* New Delhi: Arnold-Heinemann, 1975.

______. *An Apology for Heroism: A Brief Autobiography:* New Delhi: Arnold-Heinemann, 1975.

Bhattacharya, Bhabani. *So Many Hungers!* New Delhi: Orient Paperbacks, 1973.

Brecht, Bertolt. *Mother Courage and Her Childern,* ed. Bently. Metheun, 1962.

Chattopadhyaya, Harindranath. *Five Plays.* Pondicherry, 1937.

Currimbhoy, Asif. *The Hungry Ones.* Calcutta: Writers Workshop, 1977.

______. *Inquilab.* Calcutta: Writers Workshop, 1971.

Das, Gurcharan. *Larins Sahib.* Delhi: Oxford University Press, 1970.

Sarabhai, Bharathi. *The Well of the People.* Calcutta: Viswa Bharati, 1943.

Sircar Badal. *Bhoma.* Trans. Badal Sircar and Kalyani Ghosh in *Three Plays.* Calcutta: Seagull Books, 1983.

______. *Procession.* Trans. Samik Bandyopadhyay. Calcutta: Seagull Books, 1983.

Tagore, Rabindranath. *The Red Oleander.* Madras: Macmillan India, 1973.

SECONDARY SOURCES

A. ARTICLES

Abbas, K.A. " Social Realism and Change." *Aspects of Indian Literature: The Changing Pattern*, ed. Suresh Kohli. Delhi: Vikas, 1975. 145-54.

Anand, Shahla. "Folk Element and Theatre in India." *Journal of South Asian Review*, Vol. 4, No. 2.

Aravamudhan, Gita. "Traps of Tradition," *The Hindu* (Sunday Magazine), 1993.

Bandyopadhyay, Sarit Kumar. "Trends in Modern Bengali Drama." *Indian Writing Today*, 13, Vol. IV, No. 3 (1970): 149-55.

Bayapa Reddy, P. "The Bengal Trilogy." *The Plays of Asif Currimbhoy*. Calcutta: A Writer's Book, 1985: 31-52.

Benerjee, Sumantha, "Sting of Betrayal, " *Economic and Political Weekly* (5 Feb. 1983): 175-77.

Bhatta, S.K. "Epic Themes in Indo-English Plays." *Triveni*, Vol. 49, No. 4 (Jan.-March 1981): 43-52.

Bhattacharya, Asutosh. "Indian Folk Literature with Special Reference to Bengali Literature." *Indian Literature*, ed. Arabinda Poddar. 137-47.

Bhattacharya, V. "Bengali." *Contemporary Indian Literature and Society*, ed. Jotwani. New Delhi: Heritage, 1979: 18-49.

Bhatnagar, O.P "Feminism in Snehalatha Reddy's 'Sita': An Indian Play in English." *The Literary Endeavour*, Vol. I, No. 3 (1989).

Bose, Amalendu. "The Tides Flow on." *Indian Literature*, Vol. XXIII, No. 6, 1986: 181-94.

Chakraborty, M. "Trends in Recent Bengali Drama." *Indian Literature*, 24, 111 (1981).

Chatterjee, Margaret. "Social Political Ideas in Nineteenth and Twentieth Century Bengali Literature." *Indian Literature*, ed. Poddar. 262-70.

Choudhuri, Indranath. "Indianness in Indian Literature." *Comparative Indian Literature: Some Perspectives*. New Delhi: Sterling, 1992: 24-40.

______. "The Sociology of Drama and the Problem of Aesthetic Value in Modern Hindi and Bengali Theatre." *Comparative Indain Literature*, 183-95.

Das Gupta, Alokranjan. "Bengali." *Indian Literature since Independence: A Symposium*, ed. K.R.S. Iyengar. New Delhi: Sahitya Akademi, 1973: 10-26.

Devi, G.N. "Confrontation with Society." *The Hindu* (Sunday), 1 Aug. 1993: xii.

Garg, Mridula "The Security Syndrome in Modern Hindi Story." *The Book Reivew*, Vol. XVII, No. 9 (Sept. 1993), 14-50.

Ghose, S.K. "Bengali Literature Today." *Indian Literature*, ed. Poddar.

Goyal, Bhagwat S. "Indo-English." *Contemporary Indian Literature and Society*, ed. Jotwani. New Delhi: Heritage, 1979: 32-49.

Guha, Ranjit. "The Prose of Counter-Insurgency," *Subaltern Studies II*, ed. Guha. Delhi: Sahitya Akademi, 1973: 1983: 1-42

Iyengar, K.R.S. Introduction. *Indian Literature since Independence*. New Delhi: Sahitya Akademi, 1973: vii-xiv.

Jain, Jasbir. "The Feminist Perspective: The Indian Situation and its Literary Manifestations." *Problems of Post Colonial Literatures and Other Essays*. Jaipur: Printwell, 1991: 29-39.

Kennedy, Richard S. "Attitudes towards the Independent Women in Five

Bengali Novels." *Indian Literature,* Vol. XXII, No. 4 (1970): 145-66.

Kyi, Aung San Suu. "Freedom from Fear." *The Hindu*, 28 Feb. 1993: ii.

Lowenthal, Leo. "Motifs in the Realistic Plays." *Ibsen: A Collection of Critical Essays*, ed. Rolf FJELDE. New Jersey: Prentice-Hall, Englewood Cliffs, 1965: 139-57.

MacCabe, Colin. Foreword. *In Other Worlds: Essays on Cultural Politics* by Gayatri Chakraborty Spivak. New York and London: Methuen, 1987: ix-xix.

Machwe, Prabhakar. "Drama: A Search for Modern Idiom." *Four Decades of Indian Lilterature: A Critical Evaluation*. New Delhi: Chetana, 1976: 126-38.

Naik, M.K. "The Achievement of Indian English Drama." *Dimensions of Indian English Literature,* ed. Naik. New Delhi: Sterling, 1984: 151-65.

Paul, Rajinder. "Modern Indian Theatare." *The Book Review*, Vol. XIV, No. 2 (1990): 30-31.

Poddar, Arabinda. "Lord Byron and the Literary Renaissance in Bengali." *Indian Literature*, ed. Poddar. Simla: Institute of Advanced Study, 1972: 116-26.

Sen, Jai. "The Unintended City." *Seminar*, 200 (April, 1976): 33-40.

Sen, Sukumar. "The Western Stage and the Early Days of the Bengali Drama." *History of Bengali Literature*, ed. Sukumar Sen. New Delhi: Sahitya Akademi, 1960: 175-85.

Sinha, Arun. "Violence against Poor." *Economic Political Weekly,* Vol. XII, No. 15 (1977): 594.

Sundararaman, M.N. "Tradition and Modernity in Indian English Drama." *Journal of Indian Writing in English*, Vol. 20, Nos. 1 & 2 (Jan.–July, 1992).

Sutherland, Valerie. "Postmodernist Strategies in Janet Frame's *Scented Gardens for the Blind*." *The Commonwealth Review,* Vol. III (1991-92): 121-34.

Vajpeyi, Kailash. "Social Realism and Change." *Aspects of Indian Literature: A Changing Pattern,* ed. Suresh Kohli. New Delhi: Vikas, 1975: 150-70.

"Witchcraft." *Dictionary of the History of Ideas IV*, ed. Philip P. Wiener. New York: Charles Scribner's Sons, 1973: 521.

B. BOOKS

Anand, Mulk Raj. *The Indian Theatre.* London: Dennis Dobson, 1950.

Anniah Gowda, H.H. *Indian Drama*. Mysore, 1974.

Axton, Marie, et al. *English Drama: Forms and Development*. Cambridge University Press, 1977.

Bacon, Wallace A. *The Art of Interpretation.* New York: Holt, Rinehart and Winston, 1972.

Bayyapa Reddy, P. *The Plays of Asif Currimbhoy*. Calcutta: A Writer's Workshop, 1985.

Benegal, Som. *A Panorama of Theatre in India*. New Delhi: Indian Council for Cultural Relations, 1967.

Bently, Eric. *What is Theatre?* London: Methuen, 1969.

Bhatta, S.K. *Indian English Drama: A Critical Study*. New Delhi: Sterling, 1987.

Bagard, Tarvis, et al. *Modern Drama: Essays in Criticism*. London: Oxford University Press, 1971.

Brooks, Cleanth, et al. *Understanding Drama*. London: Penguin, 1972.

Choudhuri, A.D. *Contemporary British Drama: An Outsider's View*. New Delhi: Arnold-Heinemann, 1976.

Choudhuri, Indranath. *Comparative Indian Literature: Some Perspectives*. New Delhi: Sterling, 1992.

Craig, E.G. *On the Art of the Theatre*. London, 1911.

Curry, Jennifer. *Amateur Theatre*. Great Britain: Hodder and Stoughton, 1980.

Daiches, David. *Critical Approaches to Literature*. Bombay: Orient Longman, 1977.

Dass, Veena Noble. *Modern Indian Drama in English Translation*. Hyderabad: Taurus, 1988.

Duroke, Bernard F. *Harold Pinter*. London: Macmillan, 1982.

Eagleton, Terry. *Marxism and Literary Criticism*. London: Methuen, 1976.

Eisenstein, Zillah R., ed. *Capitalist Patriarchy and the Case for Socialist Feminism*. New York Monthly Review Press, 1979.

Ellis9-Fermor, Una. *The Frontiers of Drama*. London: Methuen, 1948.

Gargi, Balwant. *Folk Theatre of India*. Seatle University of Washington Press, 1966.

______. *Theatre in India*. New York: Theatre Art Books, 1962.

Gascoigne, Bamber. *Twentieth-Century Drama*. London: Hutchinson University Library, 1974.

Gupta, Balarama G.S. *Essays on Indian Writing in English*. Gulbarga: JIWE Publications, 1975.

Gupta, Hemendranath Das. *The Indian Theatre*. Delhi: Gian, 1988.

Iyengar. K.R.S., ed. *Drama in Modern India and the Writer's Responsibility in a Rapidly Changing World*. Bombay: The P.E.N. All Indian Centre, 1961.

______. *Indian Literature since Independence*. New Delhi: Sahitya Akademi, 1973.

______. *Indian Writing in English*. New Delhi: Sterling, 1984.

Kamble. N.D. *Bonded Labour in India*. New Delhi: Uppal, 1982.

Levi, Sylvan. *The Theatre of India*, 2 Vol. Calcutta: Writer's Workshop, 1978.

MacCutchion, David. *Indian Writing in English: Critical Essays*. New Delhi: Chetana, 1978.

Machwe, Prabhakar. *Modernity and Contemporary Indian Literature*. New Delhi: Chetana, 1979.

______. *Four Decades of Indian Literature: A Critical Evaluation*. New Delhi: Chetana, 1976.

Mathur, J.C. *Drama in Rural India*. New York: Asia, 1964.

______. *Themes in Indo-Anglian Literature* Bareilly: Prakash, 1971.

Mukherjee, Meenakshi. *The Twice-Born Fiction*. New Delhi: Arnold-Heinemann, 1971.

Naik, M.K. *Critical Essays on Indian Writing in English*. Madras: Macmillan.

Naik, M.K. and S. Mokashi-Punekar, ed. *Perspectives on Indian Drama in English*. Madras: Oxford University Press, 1977.

Narasimhaiah, C.D. *The Swan and the Eagle*. Simla: Indian Institute of Advanced Study, 1969.

Nazareth, Peter. *The Third World Writer: His Social Responsibility*. Nairobi: Kenya Literature Bureau, 1978.

Prasad, Brijraj. *A Background to the Study of English Literature*. Madras: Macmillan, 1978.

Raha, Kironmoy. *Bengal Theatre*. New Delhi: NBT, 1978.

Rangacharya, Adya. *The Indian Theatre*. New Delhi: NBT, 1971.

Read, Herbert. *The Meaning of Art*. London: Faber & Faber, 1984.

Ruthven, K.K., *Feminist Literary Studies: An Introduction*. Cambridge University Press, 1984.

Shah, Kalpana. *Women's Liberation and Voluntary Action*. Delhi: Ajanta, 1984.

Sharma, K.K., ed. *Indo-Englsih Literature*. Ghaziabad: Vimal, 1977.

Sircar, Badal. *The Third Theatre*. Calcutta, 1978.

Styan, J.L. *The Elements of Drama*. New Delhi: Vikas, 1979.

______. *Drama, Stage and Audience*. Cambridge University Press, 1975.

Tharu, Susie and K. Lalitha. *Women Writing in India*, Vol. II. New York: Feminist Press, 1993.

Verghese, Paul. *Essays on Indian Writing in English*. New Delhi: N.V. Publications, 1975.

______. *Problems of the Indian Creative Writer in English*. Bombay: Somaiya, 1971.

Watson, G.J. *Drama: An Introduction*. London: Macmillan Education, 1983.

Wilson, H.H., et al. *The Theatre of the Hindus*. Calcutta: Susil Gupta, 1955.

Williams, H.M. *Indo-Anglian Literature 1800-1970: A Study*. Bangalore: Orient Longman, 1976.

Index

Aajir 24, 25, 27, 46-63, 64, 65, 68, 78, 82, 85, 87, 92, 104, 105, 107, 127, 129
Abbas, K.A. 10, 28n, 67, 81n
Agnigarbha 17, 22, 30
Amritha Sanchay 18
Anand, Mulk Raj 48, 55, 61
Andharmanik 18
Aranyer Adhikar 15, 16, 18, 22
Aravamudan, Geeta 103n
Aurobindo, Sri 8, 125

Baki Itihas 14
Banarjee, Sumantha 40, 45n
Bandyopadhyay, Samik 11, 17, 23, 24, 28n, 30, 45n, 53, 63n, 65, 73, 81n, 103n, 105n, 125n, 126, 132n
Bandyopadhyay, Sarit Kumar 10, 28n
Bandyopadhyay, Tarashankar 19
Basumathi 20
Bayen 24, 25, 27, 82-103, 104, 107, 109, 112, 127, 129
Beckett, Samuel 14
Bhaduri, Satinath 19
Bhatta, S.K. 28n
Bhattacharya, Bijan 10, 16
Bhoma 18
Bonded Labour in India 47, 63n
Bose, Asit 30
Brecht, Bertolt 49, 89, 127

Cabe, Colin Mac 29n
Chakraborty, Kavikankan Mukundaram 18, 19, 20
'Champa' 46
Chandalika Panchali 19
Chandra, Sarat 18
Chandra, Shibik 53
Chatterjee, Margaret 28
Chattopadhyay, Harindranath 8
Chotti Munda O Tar Teer 30
Choudhury, Indranath 9, 28n
'Constructive Critique' 21
Coolie 55
'cultural exhibit' 21
Currimbhoy, Asif 11, 12, 30, 36, 74, 125

Dass, Veena Noble 13, 28n
Desh 20
Devy, G.N. 23
'Dewana' 46
Dheebar 46
Doldrummers 12
'dramatized documents' 24
'Draupadi' 21, 22
'Drushya Kavya' 15
Dumb Dancer, The 12
Dutt, Michael Madhusudan 7, 125

Evam Indrajit 14

'Fifth Veda' 7, 125
'Freedom from Fear' 63n
Freud, Sigmund 87

Guha, Ranjit 48, 63n
Gupta, Asit 8

Hayavadana 13
Hindu 63n
Hungry Ones 74

Inquilab 12, 30, 36
IPTA 125
"Is This Called Civilization?" 7, 125

Iyengar, K.R. Srinivasa 27n, 28n

'Jawl' 104
Jayashree 20
Jhansir Ranee 18
Juganthar 16
Kailasam, T.P. 8, 125
Kamble, N.D. 47
Karnad, Girish 8, 11, 12, 13, 15, 125
'Khoimala' 46
Kohli, Suresh 28n
Kyi, Aung San Suu 55, 71

Lalitha, K. 22
'Laila Majnu' 77

Machwe, Prabhakar 10, 28n
Mahabharata, The 8, 52
Michhil 54
Mokashi-Punekar, S. 127, 132n
Mother of 1084 24, 26, 30-45, 46, 50, 64, 67, 82, 83, 86, 92, 100, 105, 112, 128, 129
Mukherjee, Sujit 30, 45n

Nabanna 10, 15
Naik, M.K. 7, 8, 27n, 126, 132n
Nandy, Pritish 28n
Narasimhaiah, C.D. 63n

Operation? Bashai Tudu 52
'Organic Intellectual' 93

Paul, Rajinder 12, 14, 28n
'Pindadan' 46
Pinter, Harold 14
'Pterodectyle' 21

Rakasi Kora 126
Ramayana, The 8
Red Oleanders, The 74, 81n
Refugee, The 12

Sakharam Binder 13
Sarabhai, Bharathi 113
Seagull Theatre Quarterly 126, 133n
Seminar 81n, 129n
Sen, Jai 69
Shakespeare, William 7
'Shareer' 46
Silence, the Court is in Session 13
Sinha, Arun 81n
Sircar, Badal 11, 14, 15, 54, 62n, 67, 81n, 125, 127
Sonar Bangla 12
Spivak, Gayatri Chakraborty 18, 19, 21, 28n, 45n, 48, 62n, 93
'Stanadayini' 46, 99
'Sting of Betrayal' 40
Sundararaman, M.N. 8, 28n
Sutherland, Valerie 103n
Swan and the Eagle, The 62n

Tagore, Rabindranath 15, 18, 74, 81n
Tendulkar, Vijay 11, 13, 15, 125
Todd, Janet 23, 29n
'Traps of Tradition' 103n
Tughlaq 12, 13

Urvashi O Johnny 24, 25, 27, 64-81, 105, 129, 130
Untouchable 48
Udayam 63n, 125
'Unintended City' 81n
'Untapped Resources' 108, 132n

Venugopal, C.V. 28n, 34 45n
Venugopal, N. 103n

Water 24, 26, 27, 104-25, 128, 129, 131
Watson, G.J. 63n
Waugh, Patricia 97
Well of the People, The 121
Wesker, Arnold 127
'Witchcraft' 103n
'Witchcraft Persecution' 84
'Wrong Number' 46

'Yaksha Town' 74
Yayati 16